LIFE
WITHOUT
DEFEAT

THE
POWER
IN THE
OVERCOMING LIFE

BOOK 1

A Lead Right Consulting Book

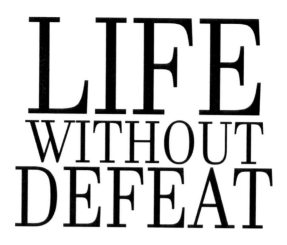

LIFE WITHOUT DEFEAT

THE
POWER
IN THE
OVERCOMING LIFE

BOOK 1

Ezekiel Leke Ojo

GODKULTURE
PUBLISHING

Published by Godkulture Publishing.

ISBN 978-0-9904637-4-0
eBook ISBN 978-0-9904637-5-7
Library of Congress Number 2015952981

Unless otherwise stated, all scriptures are taken from the King James Version © 1982 by Thomas Nelson, Inc.

Cover Design by Rotimi Kehinde
Cover Photo 'Victory' by Oren Gelbendorf

Printed in the United States of America

Dedication

This book is dedicated to everyone that cherishes the victory of light over darkness.

Content

Foreword

The Bible says *"You are of God, little children, and have overcome them, because He who is in you is greater than he who is in the world."* (1John 4:4)

Ignorance of the mystery of the overcoming life, the LIFE WITHOUT DEFEAT, is a tragedy of Christianity. God's people perish because of lack of understanding of that "Who" that is in them that is greater than he who is in the world.

This book is a practical, brilliant and successful effort aimed at destroying the root of ignorance of the truth that sets people free.

The author takes the reader through a great journey of who we are in Christ, the blessings and benefits of living a life in the Spirit and how to be empowered by the Holy Spirit to live a life without defeat.

This book is a must read for all those who desire to truly live life without defeat. I know you are one of them and I wholly recommend this great book to you. Be richly blessed as you read!

Pastor Leke Sanusi,
Author, Conference Speaker

Acknowledgements

I never knew writing a book was more difficult than preaching a message until I embarked on this journey. Indeed it has been a long and experienced-filled journey. Thank God for the final product.

I did not get to this point alone, many people have been of assistance in one way or the other and they deserve to be acknowledged.

First is the Almighty God without whom there will be no grace to do anything - John 15:5. Paul, writing to the church in Corinth, said in 1 Corinthians 3:6-7 that, "*I have planted, Apollos watered; but God gave the increase. So then neither is he that planteth anything, neither he that watereth; but God that giveth the increase.*" I give Him praise for everything.

Second is my wife of 18years, Dr Olajuyi Ebunoluwa Ojo, who indeed has been a gift to me all the way. The encouragement, the touch of class and the continuous nudging and criticisms made invaluable contributions to the whole process.

Third is Pastor James Nyema, the Presiding Pastor of African Faith Expression Ministries in Phoenix Arizona whose book launch ceremony propelled me to discharge some "stuff" that has been laying within me.

Next is my staff at RCCG Solid Rock Phoenix. Deacon Amo Acheampong, my Personal Assistant and Pastor Yomi Adewunmi, the Ministry Administrator. Your help and encouragement have been very valuable. Also, Dr Lola Faleye who has been helping to make this a reality, I salute you.

Mr. Rotimi Kehinde of GodKulture Publishing, for giving life back to a dying project, I commend you.

All the members and leaders in RCCG Solid Rock Phoenix, for patiently listening to my messages and encouraging me to push on for the past 13 years.

And to all my mentors, mentees and colleagues in ministry who are too many to mention, I thank you for all your help and support.

And finally to David and Debbie Ojo, my beloved biological children, you are the best.

Endorsements

This book, The Life Without Defeat - Power in the Overcoming Life, gives us the critical understanding of the power of the sacrifice made for us by Jesus Christ and ensuing authority and the power that we have access to as Christians.

There are practical things in this book expressed by the writer on how to live a life of the spirit and the things that can give us the edge we need to live a daily victorious life in Christ. For those that long to enjoy true success and victory in all areas of life, I recommend that you take time to read this book.

Thank you Pastor Ezekiel Leke Ojo for taking time to write this wonderful masterpiece. It is a timeless portion and worth reading.

Michael Ibukun Olotu,
RCCG Cornerstone Worship Center, Chandler AZ

Introduction

❧

It has always been the desire of every man to be great and successful. The journey of man has always been how to get fulfilled in life. Our daily life pursuits have always been centered on success, greatness and fulfillment. Many decisions taken by man are always geared towards the accomplishment of the above three objectives. Questions bordering on where to live, whom to marry, what career to pursue and more arise daily. God is not against man achieving these three objectives. That is why the Bible says in Jeremiah 29:11 *"For I know the thoughts that I think toward you, saith the Lord, thoughts of peace, and not of evil, to give you an expected end."*

More than man wants to prosper, God wants man to have all-round prosperity. That is why the Bible says in 3 John 2 *"Beloved, I wish above all things that thou mayest prosper and be in health, even as thy soul prospereth."*

Men always have at the back of their minds the fulfillment of these three objectives. Unfortunately, in the course of pursuing these objectives which in themselves are not sinful, man has always failed to properly answer the "how" question.

How can I be successful?
How can I be great?
How can I be fulfilled in life?

The answers to the above questions from a believer must definitely be different from the rest of the world. Romans 8:1-13 captures the answer:

"There is therefore now no condemnation to them which are in Christ Jesus, who walk not after the flesh, but after the Spirit. For the law of the Spirit of life in Christ Jesus hath made me free from the law of sin and death. For what the law could not do, in that it was weak through the flesh, God sending his own Son in the likeness of sinful flesh, and for sin, condemned sin in the flesh: That the righteousness of the law might be fulfilled in us, who walk not after the flesh, but after the Spirit. For they that are after the flesh do mind the things of the flesh; but they that are after the Spirit the things of the Spirit. For to be carnally minded is death; but to be spiritually minded is life and peace. Because the carnal mind is enmity against God: for it is not subject to the law of God, neither indeed can be. So then they that are in the flesh cannot please God. But ye are not in the flesh, but in the Spirit, if so be that the Spirit of God dwell in you. Now if any man has not the Spirit of Christ, he is none of his. And if Christ be in you, the body is dead because of sin; but the Spirit is life because of righteousness. But if the Spirit of him that raised up Jesus from the dead dwell in you, he that raised up Christ from the dead shall also quicken your mortal bodies by his Spirit that dwelleth in you. Therefore, brethren, we are debtors, not to the flesh, to live after the flesh. For if ye live after the flesh, ye shall die: but if ye through the Spirit do mortify the deeds of the body, ye shall live."

The answer from the above scriptures is simple: The Spirit of God must govern your life.

In this book, I have written from my heart and from the Scriptures to help you understand how to live a fulfilled life, a life that is beyond the ordinary; a Spirit-led life. An overcoming life does not conform to the fears and cares of this world and produces amazing results beyond human effort. Through the empowerment of the Holy Spirit, you can grasp this potent concept of living the overcoming life.

Be blessed.

Ezekiel Leke Ojo

Chapter 1

Christ-Centered Life

❦

There is therefore now no condemnation to those who are in Christ Jesus, who do not walk according to the flesh, but according to the Spirit. For the law of the Spirit of life in Christ Jesus has made me free from the law of sin and death. For what the law could not do in that it was weak through the flesh, God did by sending His own Son in the likeness of sinful flesh, on account of sin: He condemned sin in the flesh, that the righteous requirement of the law might be fulfilled in us who do not walk according to the flesh but according to the Spirit. (Romans 8:1-4)

You cannot understand what it means to walk in the spirit if you do not understand what it means to be born of the Spirit. The events of Genesis chapters 1 and 2 refer only to the creation of man and how man became a living soul when God breathed life into him. Yet, every one accepting Jesus Christ as Savior must go through two different births in a lifetime. The first one is the natural birth and the second, the spiritual birth.

Every man given birth to by a woman was shaped in iniquity and conceived in sin as stated in Psalm 51:5 that *"Behold, I was brought forth in iniquity, And in sin my mother conceived me."* So, we all have sinned, and come short of the glory of God. Obviously, the natural birth comes with a burden of sin and condemnation. Thus, for man to fulfill his divine purpose there must be another birth for God cannot partner with a sinner. Then, how can a man be born of the spirit?

Nicodemus' encounter with Jesus as illustrated in John 3:1-8 is a good introduction to that spiritual experience. Nicodemus asked a purely natural question because his spirit was dead to spiritual matters, "How can a man be born when he is old? Can he enter a second time into his mother's womb and be born?" Jesus answered him in accordance to the Pharisee's teaching because he was one.

The Pharisees believed that being born physically meant to be born of water. This was implied by Nicodemus remark who interpreted physical birth as being born again. In verse 5, Jesus told him, "Unless one is born of water and the Spirit, you cannot enter the kingdom of God."

Nicodemus believed like the other Jews that because he was born a Jew and kept God's ordinances, he should automatically enter into the kingdom of God. On the other hand, Jesus explained this is not enough. Our Lord Jesus Christ interprets the water as flesh (a physical birth), "That which is born of the flesh is flesh, and that which is born of the Spirit is spirit." He told Nicodemus that though he had already been given birth to physically but he still needed to be reborn spiritually.

SPIRITUAL DEVELOPMENT

The new birth ushers into the spirit of believers, eternal life. How can a believer progress from this new birth to walking in the spirit? Just as it is impossible for a naturally new born baby to begin walking immediately, it is also not possible for a newly born again Christian to start walking in the spirit instantly. They both go through a process of transiting from one level to the next. There are two steps to walking in the spirit. The first step is to allow the limbs to grow which gradually leads to the second step of starting to walk well.

As newborn babes, desire the pure milk of the word that you may grow thereby. (1 Peter 2:2)

A natural baby starts taking milk in order to grow his members. So likewise, the newly born again Christian also requires the milk of the Word to grow spiritually. The natural babe cannot walk except the limbs start to grow; so likewise the new believer cannot start to walk until his spiritual limbs begin to develop as a result of nourishment through the Word. The milk will strengthen the limbs; however, over time, skills are necessary so as not to fall while walking.

Developing these skills requires regular intake of strong meat of the Word as prescribed by Paul in Hebrews 5:11-14. At this level, the believer understands the voice and language of the Spirit, and begins to walk in the Spirit, discerning between good and evil.

For the law of the Spirit of life in Christ Jesus has made me free from the law of sin and death. For what the law could not do in that it was weak through the flesh, God did by sending His own Son in the likeness of sinful flesh, on account of sin: He condemned sin in the flesh. (Romans 8:2-3)

Walking in the Spirit is a deliberate focus on the Lord and His Word, not yielding to the flesh but rather following the guidance of the Holy Spirit. In the process of yielding to the Spirit, a believer might be entangled with the yoke of bondage and return to sin, thereby falling under the law.

What is a law? A law is a set of rules and guidelines, which are enforced through social institutions to govern human behavior. Both the law of sin and death and the law of the spirit of life in Christ Jesus at some point govern all human beings. There is a constant war between the spirit and the flesh. And if man continually operates under the law of sin and death, there is no hope for restoration with God. However, because of what Christ did at Calvary, believers are not counted guilty and will not be punished on the day of judgment so far they repent when they err.

This is hard to believe, because we know that sin deserves to be punished. Nevertheless, the gospel announced that Christ has taken our sins, and the consequences, on Himself. He has experienced the consequences of sin, and escaped, so that we can also escape. On behalf of all humanity, Christ has experienced the results of our sins, so there is no further condemnation waiting for us. If we trust Him, if our lives are in Him, we do not need to be afraid.

LIFE VERSUS DEATH

By His Spirit working inside of us, we cannot be under the bondage of any law because Jesus has made us free from the law of sin and death, the only law that could possibly condemn us. The law that says, "Those who sin shall die," no longer applies to us, because it has been done away with. We died with Christ, and it is no longer we who sin, but it's the sinful nature inside of us that does it (Romans 7:17). The law could not give us eternal life, but God could, and He did it through the death of Christ.

For what the law could not do in that it was weak through the flesh, God did by sending His own Son in the likeness of sinful flesh, on account of sin: He condemned sin in the flesh. (Romans 8:3)

For those who live according to the flesh set their minds on the things of the flesh, but those who live according to the Spirit, the things of the Spirit. For to be carnally minded is death, but to be spiritually minded is life and peace. Because the carnal mind is enmity against God; for it is not subject to the law of God, nor indeed can be. So then, those who are in the flesh cannot please God. But you are not in the flesh but in the Spirit, if indeed the Spirit of God dwells in you. Now if anyone does not have the Spirit of Christ, he is not His. And if Christ is in you, the body is dead because of sin, but the Spirit is life because of righteousness. But if the Spirit of Him who raised Jesus from the dead dwells in you, He who raised Christ from the dead will also give life to your mortal bodies through His Spirit who dwells in you. (Romans 8:5-11)

We do not live according to the flesh but according to the Spirit. We do not set our minds on what the flesh wants but on what the Spirit desires. We are not perfect, but as the Spirit leads us, we think and do the things of God.

The unconverted mind "is hostile to God. It does not submit to God's law, nor can it do so." It is rebellious and disobedient. Those who operate in the realm of the flesh cannot please God. If you are struggling with the flesh, ask God to deliver you so you can begin to follow the leading of the Spirit.

The Holy Spirit lives in and guides everyone who belongs to Christ, and "the mind governed by the Spirit is life and peace. Therefore, cooperate with Him, He can accomplish a lot through you.

CARNALITY

The book of Romans chapter eight clearly distinguishes between the two possible governments that man is subject to: the carnal and spirit government. Let's look at four of the components of carnality, namely: old man, flesh, carnal and sin.

The Old Man: The phrase, "the old man" refers to our source of corruption, which dates back to Adam. The old man refers to the total unregenerate person and his reprobate nature, which was as a result of his connection with Adam. It is who we were before being saved; the old man relates us back to Adam, just as the new man relates us back to Christ

That you put off, concerning your former conduct, the old man which grows corrupt according to the deceitful lusts. (Ephesians 4:22)

Carnal: The word "carnal" is translated from the Greek word, *sarkikos,* which literally means "fleshly." According to the Greek dictionary, it means to have the nature and characteristics of the flesh or simply put, "fleshly." It refers to "man's natural disposition to sin" and to oppose or do away with God. Other synonyms for the word, carnal are flesh, sinful nature, Adamic nature.

And I, brethren, could not speak to you as to spiritual people but as to carnal, as to babes in Christ. (1 Corinthians 3:1)

The Flesh: The Biblical term "flesh," refers to what we are in God's sight because of Adam's sin. Thus, it goes further to denote man's own effort independent of God. The flesh is the sum total of all of man's personality from his corrupt nature. A man operates in the flesh because his mind is darkened, as a result of his alienation from God. The flesh also refers to helplessness, impotence, or weakness (Romans 8:3, Romans 6:19). The physical body in itself is not sinful; rather, it is the vehicle through which sin operates to translate its desires into deeds.

For when we were in the flesh, the sinful passions which were aroused by the law were at work in our members to bear fruit to death. (Romans 7:5)

Sin: The term "sin" refers to the state in which all men are born because of Adam's sin. Of course, sin is referred to as an act that flows from the sinful nature. Sin is that basic nature we have as *adamic* beings. It also connotes the essential nature resident within us because of the fall of man.

If we say that we have no sin, we deceive ourselves, and the truth is not in us. (1 John 1:8)

This suffices that we have a nature within us that God calls sin, which we refer to as 'the sinful nature.' Thus, we can safely conclude that carnality is a state in which our bodies serve as an instrument through which sin finds expression. We derived this nature from Adam; hence, it's referred to as the old man. All that flows from it is sinful according to Galatians 5:19-21 which says "*Now the works of the flesh are evident, which are: adultery, fornication, uncleanness, lewdness, idolatry, sorcery, hatred, contentions, jealousies, outbursts of wrath, selfish ambitions, dissensions, heresies, envy, murders, drunkenness, revelries, and the like; of which I tell you beforehand, just as I also told you in time past, that those who practice such things will not inherit the kingdom of God."*

It is perilous to continue in carnality. Thus yield your members unto God so you can bear the fruit of righteousness.

The attributes of a carnal man are as follows:

1. His mind is focused on the things of the flesh. His life is filled with passion and lust for the mundane issues of life.

   For those who live according to the flesh set their minds on the things of the flesh, but those who live according to the Spirit, the things of the Spirit. (Romans 8:5)

   Among whom also we all once conducted ourselves in the lusts of our flesh, fulfilling the desires of the flesh and of the mind, and were by nature children of wrath, just as the others. (Ephesians 2:3)

   For all that is in the world—the lust of the flesh, the lust of the eyes, and the pride of life—is not of the Father but is of the world. (1 John 2:16)

2. He is enslaved by his own desires

   I thank God—through Jesus Christ our Lord! So then, with the mind I myself serve the law of God, but with the flesh the law of sin. (Romans 7:25)

3. Cannot be God's friend as he is not subject to His laws

   Because the carnal mind is enmity against God; for it is not subject to the law of God, nor indeed can be. (Romans 8:7)

4. Cannot please God no matter how hard he tries

So then, those who are in the flesh cannot please God. (Romans 8:8)

5. A carnal man is self-centered. He only thinks about his own pleasure.

BIBLICAL EXAMPLES OF CARNAL MEN

The Rich Young Ruler:

He came to Jesus wanting to know how he can inherit eternal life. He tried to convince Jesus that he had observed all that was written in the books. And Jesus asked him a question to know where his heart was, advised him to sell all his possessions, carry his cross and follow him. Nonetheless, the man became sad because he could not do away with his possessions. He walked away dejectedly.

Now as He was going out on the road, one came running, knelt before Him, and asked Him, "Good Teacher, what shall I do that I may inherit eternal life?" So Jesus said to him, "Why do you call Me good? No one is good but One, that is, God. You know the commandments: 'Do not commit adultery,' 'Do not murder,' 'Do not steal,' 'Do not bear false witness,' 'Do not defraud,' 'Honor your father and your mother.'"

And he answered and said to Him, "Teacher, all these things I have kept from my youth." Then Jesus, looking at him, loved him, and said to him, "One thing you lack: Go your way, sell whatever you have and give to the poor, and you will have treasure in heaven; and come, take up the cross, and follow Me." But he was sad at this word, and went away sorrowful, for he had great possessions. (Mark 10:17-22)

The Rich Fool:

And He said to them, "Take heed and beware of covetousness, for one's life does not consist in the abundance of the things he possesses." Then He spoke a parable to them, saying: "The ground of a certain rich man yielded plentifully. And he thought within himself, saying, 'What shall I do, since I have no room to store my crops?' So he said, 'I will do this: I will pull down my barns and build greater, and there I will store all my crops and my goods. And I will say to my soul, "Soul, you have many goods laid up for many years; take your ease; eat, drink, and be merry."' But God said to him, 'Fool! This night your soul will be required of you; then whose will those things be which you have provided?' "So is he who lays up treasure for himself, and is not rich toward God." (Luke 12:15-21)

A carnal man is self-centered. He only thinks about his own pleasure. One of the ways to know how carnal you have become is the extent to which you covet material things above the spiritual. The rich fool was consumed all the while with his riches and what he planned to do with them. This carnal man thought the whole world was at his feet, not knowing that he was spiritually dead.

However, verse 20 of Luke 12 shows the vanity of a carnal life, *"But God said to him, 'Fool! This night your soul will be required of you; then whose will those things be which you have provided?'"* (Luke 12:13-21)

WALKING IN THE SPIRIT

I say then: Walk in the Spirit, and you shall not fulfill the lust of the flesh. For the flesh lusts against the Spirit, and the Spirit against the flesh; and these are contrary to one another, so that you do not do the things that you wish. But if you are led by the Spirit, you are not under the law. Now the works of the flesh are evident, which are: adultery, fornication, uncleanness, lewdness, idolatry, sorcery, hatred, contentions, jealousies, outbursts of wrath, selfish ambitions, dissensions, heresies, envy, murders, drunkenness, revelries, and the like; of which I tell you beforehand, just as I also told you in time past, that those who practice such things will not inherit the kingdom of God. But the fruit of the Spirit is love, joy, peace, longsuffering, kindness, goodness, faithfulness, gentleness, self-control. Against such there is no law. And those who are Christ's have crucified the flesh with its passions and desires. If we live in the Spirit, let us also walk in the Spirit. Let us not become conceited, provoking one another, envying one another. (Galatians 5:16-26)

Different components of carnality have been talked about. What can believers do not to always fall into the lustful desires of the flesh? This is of great necessity if they are to fulfill God's will. Many a times, Christians allow their fleshly ways get the best of them and in doing so miss out on what is God's will for them. A group of men who were married were asked if they knew what gets on the nerves of their spouses. They all answered that they did. They were now asked, "Why then do they continue in it and make them upset? What is the benefit in that?"

On numerous occasions, we believers do things that we know are not going to reap good results. If we love God we do not even do so with determined purposes, but yet we do things in the flesh, which do not bring any benefit. As scripture says, there is nothing good that dwells in the flesh, for the flesh is opposed to God. Hence, what can we do about this? As always, God has the solution. This is one of the most important things to learn as a believer.

One of the main goals after being born again is to become more and more spiritual. This means to be controlled by the spirit, which means to be led by the Holy Spirit. The more spiritual we become, the more we are walking in the Spirit. When we do this we do not fulfill the cravings of the flesh.

The desires of the flesh apart from the Spirit of God are not going to help us in any way. If we react to people out of the flesh, we will then be habitually opposed to what God says we should do in such circumstances. This yields the fruits that none of us is proud of. If we face life's decisions and our reaction is founded off of what our flesh prompts to do, this will result in us missing out on God's will for us. Then if we want our lives to be conformed into the image of Christ and walk in the Spirit, which brings all the fruit of the Spirit, we must learn to always be controlled by the Spirit.

The way we can learn to become spiritual and not respond according to our old fleshly nature is to walk in the Spirit. This is learning to live our lives governed by the Holy Spirit who will at all times guide us in what is God's will for us, and in turn will produce godly fruit, which is far more beneficial than the works of the flesh. In the book of Galatians above, there is a list of the works of the flesh, and all we have to do is look over it and ask the Holy Spirit to help get rid of them from our lives.

It is the Spirit who gives life; the flesh profits nothing. The words that I speak to you are spirit, and they are life. (John 6:63)

Here Jesus also states that walking in the flesh will be of no benefit. He emphatically asserted that it is the Spirit who gives life, and that is the word "Zoe," which means the God-kind of life. He mentions that at the end of this verse. Did you get the message He's trying to pass across? Jesus' Words are Spirit. Hence, if we will learn to walk in light of and obedience to His Words, we will begin to walk in the Spirit.

This is where many believers have challenges. To walk in the light we must focus on what Jesus said, and what His disciples said which they learned of Him. If we are born again Christians and do not set time aside to feed on His Word, then how can we walk in the Spirit? There are two components to walking in the Word. Primarily is learning to walk in the light of God's Word, being obedient to what it says. Let's take a look at the Scripture.

If we say that we have fellowship with Him, and walk in darkness, we lie and do not practice the truth. But if we walk in the light as He is in the light, we have fellowship with one another, and the blood of Jesus Christ His Son cleanses us from all sin. (1 John 1:6-7)

Walking in the light of God's Word is practicing the truth, which is the Word of life, the Word of God. When we act on God's Word then we walk in the light as He is in the light, and we walk in the freedom that has come from the blood of Jesus, which cleansed us from all sin. Apostle James tells us that we are to be doers of the Word and not hearers only (James 1:22). A person, who hears but does not take the time to apply the Word into his life, lives a life of deception as the scripture says. So examine your ways, walk in the light of the Word by practicing what it says. We only get better in anything we embark on, provided we make a conscious effort to practice.

Therefore, if anyone is in Christ, he is a new creation; old things have passed away; behold, all things have become new. (2 Corinthians 5:17)

The second way to walking in the Word is to live with an understanding of who we are in Christ. If we do not take the time to meditate on the Word and renew our minds to who we are in Christ, we will continually think with the old fleshly mindset.

We are *not* an old sinner saved by grace. We are a *new* creation. We cannot be both. We are spiritual beings and our spirit is born again. We are a new creature all together, made in the image of God. We must gain knowledge of this or the *old fleshly nature* will keep dominating our lives.

ALIGNING WITH THE HOLY SPIRIT

For if you live according to the flesh you will die; but if by the Spirit you put to death the deeds of the body, you will live. For as many as are led by the Spirit of God, these are sons of God. For you did not receive the spirit of bondage again to fear, but you received the Spirit of adoption by whom we cry out, "Abba, Father." The Spirit Himself bears witness with our spirit that we are children of God. (Romans 8:13-16)

Walking the God-kind of life demands that His Spirit leads us. Other than that, whatever we do, we should not put this before walking in line with His Word. When talking about walking in the Spirit this is what most believers think of, being led by the Holy Spirit, and taking the Word of life for granted. However, if we are not going to feed on the Word and be strengthened to walk in the light of it, then we are not going to be in sync with the Holy Spirit. Everything He prompts us to do is always in line with God's Word.

Paul in Romans 8:13 stated that when we allow the flesh to influence our decisions and not walk in the Spirit, then we are going to have the works of the flesh manifesting. Nevertheless, when we walk in the Spirit we bear the fruit of righteousness manifested in and through us. God wants to lead us by His Spirit but His Spirit is not going to speak to our brain. As illustrated in the above scripture, His Spirit bears witness with our spirit. God is a Spirit, and He will only reveal Himself to us through our spirit. Hence, we must learn to listen to our spirit man within to follow the leading of His Spirit. How can we learn to follow the leading of the Holy Spirit?

So then, my beloved brethren, let every man be swift to hear, slow to speak, slow to wrath; for the wrath of man does not produce the righteousness of God. (James 1:19-20)

One of the ways to being led by the Spirit is to stop responding instantly to what we hear, or to what goes on around us. Be swift to hear, and slow to speak. It is our flesh that wants to instantaneously speak, and when we do so without taking time to hear what God would say in that circumstance, we end up walking in the flesh and not in the Spirit.

If we take time to hear what God is saying to us, we'll perfect the act of hearing and knowing His voice, then our lives will not be subjected to trial and error but in accordance to the leading of the Spirit. Many life's problems can be avoided this way.

Think about how different your life would be if you took the time before responding to any life's situation to simply ask the Holy Spirit, "What would God want me to say or do here?" If we will really learn this habit of listening first to our spirit man, not our thoughts or what we think, but really aligning with our spirit man within to hear from God, how different would our lives be? How different would our relationships be?

God gave us a great Helper, the Holy Spirit. However, how often do we take advantage of this great Helper to really stop and listen to what He is trying to communicate to us?

Walk in the light of the Word and listen to the Holy Spirit within you. This is how we can walk in the Spirit and thus not fulfill the desires of the flesh. Our lives will be much better, and we will experience more of God's will for us. We will walk in the fruit of the Spirit, not the works of the flesh. This is how we live a Christ-centered life. It is a much more peaceful and joyful way to live life.

Chapter 2
The Fruit of the Spirit

But the fruit of the Spirit is love, joy, peace, long suffering, gentleness, goodness, faith, Meekness, temperance: against such there is no law. And they that are Christ's have crucified the flesh with the affections and lusts. If we live in the Spirit, let us also walk in the Spirit. Let us not be desirous of vainglory, provoking one another, envying one another. (Galatians 5:22-26)

The **Fruit of the Holy Spirit** is a biblical term that sums up the nine visible attributes of a true Christian life. Though there are nine attributes to the Fruit of the Spirit, the original Greek term translated "fruit" is singular, signifying that there is one fruit with nine attributes. This is quite significant because so many people believe and teach multiple fruits of the Spirit.

In Psalm 1:1-3, the Bible says, "*Blessed is the man that walketh not in the counsel of the ungodly, nor standeth in the way of sinners, nor sitteth in the seat of the scornful. But his delight is in the law of the Lord; and in his law doth he meditate day and night. And he shall be like a tree planted by the rivers of water, that bringeth forth his fruit in his season; his leaf also shall not wither; and whatsoever he doeth shall prosper."*

You see, when you gave your life to Jesus, all the *fruit* of the Spirit were planted inside you in seed form. Through the Spirit you can experience joy and peace in every circumstance, no matter how difficult or painful.

You may not be a naturally patient person, but you can call on the Spirit within you to produce patience. If you are battling unhealthy behaviors, like an addiction or some kind of bad habit, the Holy Spirit can give you the ability to resist the devil and make healthy choices.

The apostle Paul put it this way: When we were controlled by our old nature, sinful desires were at work within us, and the law aroused these evil desires that produced a harvest of sinful deeds, resulting in death. But now we have been released from the law, for we died to it and are no longer captive to its power.

Now we can serve God, not in the old way of obeying the letter of the law, but in the new way of living in the Spirit. The Bible says in Romans 7: 5-6 that *"For when we were in the flesh, the motions of sins, which were by the law, did work in our members to bring forth fruit unto death. But now we are delivered from the law, that being dead wherein we were held; that we should serve in newness of spirit, and not in the oldness of the letter."*

On your own, it would be impossible. But when you operate in the Spirit, you have a supernatural ability to overcome sin. What a precious gift! And the more you draw near to God, praying and reflecting on His Word, the more you will experience the fruit of the Spirit in your life. But where should you start?

1. Love

All the manifestations of the fruit of the Spirit are held in place by love. Jesus said that loving God and other people is the most important commandment. Matthew 22:39 says *"You must love the LORD your God with all your heart, all your soul, and all your mind."* He added, "A second is equally important: *'Love your neighbor as yourself'."* This is commonly called "the golden rule."

Under the golden rule there are two major expectations. First is to love God and second is to love your neighbor as yourself. How do you love your neighbor? First, you must learn to receive God's love for yourself. Until then, you cannot truly love anyone else. You may do all the right things, but your motivation will be wrong. And God is not nearly as concerned about what we do as He is about the attitudes of our hearts. God loves you so much and He wants you to experience that love in the deepest part of your soul. Pray and ask Him to help you be a person who walks in love. Choose to believe the best about people rather than automatically assuming the worst.

Study the passages of Scripture that talk about God's love for you and really get them into your heart. Then ask God, "How can I encourage someone today?" Don't wait until you feel like it. Go out and love on purpose. Love must be deliberate and intentional. You must be willing and able to set aside the shortcomings of your neighbor before you can truly love him or her. You will be amazed at the joy it releases in your soul. Focus on learning to love as Jesus loved, and all the other manifestations of the fruit of the Spirit will follow.

The next question then is: How do I love God?

No man can love God without having the nature of God. Secondly, no man can love God without knowing Him. You start loving Him by imagining the works of His hands and the majesty of His personality. If you are able to actively do this you will find out that all His actions are predicated on His love. Psalm 8 is a good place to start. Without any major expectation from you, He still loved you.

Attributes of Love

The Message Bible in 1 Corinthians 13 captures the attributes of love succinctly thus:

If I speak with human eloquence and angelic ecstasy but don't love, I'm nothing but the creaking of a rusty gate. If I speak God's Word with power, revealing all his mysteries and making everything plain as day, and if I have faith that says to a mountain, "Jump," and it jumps, but I don't love, I'm nothing. If I give everything I own to the poor and even go to the stake to be burned as a martyr, but I don't love, I've gotten nowhere. So, no matter what I say, what I believe, and what I do, I'm bankrupt without love.

Love never gives up. Love cares more for others than for self. Love doesn't want what it doesn't have. Love doesn't strut, Doesn't have a swelled head, Doesn't force itself on others, Isn't always "me first," Doesn't fly off the handle, Doesn't keep score of the sins of others, Doesn't revel when others grovel, Takes pleasure in the flowering of truth, Puts up with anything, Trusts God always, Always looks for the best, Never looks back, But keeps going to the end.

Love never dies. Inspired speech will be over some day; praying in tongues will end; understanding will reach its limit. We know only a portion of the truth, and what we say about God is always incomplete. But when the Complete arrives, our incompletes will be canceled.

When I was an infant at my mother's breast, I gurgled and cooed like any infant. When I grew up, I left those infant ways for good.

We don't yet see things clearly. We're squinting in a fog, peering through a mist. But it won't be long before the weather clears and the sun shines bright! We'll see it all then, see it all as clearly as God sees us, knowing him directly just as he knows us! But for right now, until that completeness, we have three things to do to lead us toward that consummation: Trust steadily in God, hope unswervingly, love extravagantly. And the best of the three is love.

2. Joy

Webster's New World Dictionary defines *joy* as synonymous with "happy," "glad," and "cheerful." *Webster's* specifically defines it as "a very glad feeling; happiness; great pleasure; delight."

These definitions only define the expression of the wonderful emotion. They fail to consider the causes of joy, the circumstances in which it is expressed or its longevity. In these areas, the Bible presents a much more complex virtue than these definitions provide.

Biblical joy is inseparable from our relationship with God and springs from our knowledge and understanding of the purpose of life and the hope of living with God for eternity when there will be joy for evermore. If God is actually present in our lives, the joy He experiences can begin in us (Psalm 16:11). Joy is the sign that life has found its purpose, its reason for being. This, too, is a revelation of God, for no one can come to Him and find the purpose of life unless he, by his Spirit, calls Him and reveals it (John 6:44, I Corinthians 2:10).

A common mistake is to think that *getting* something will make you happy. We tell ourselves, *"If only..."* but joy and happiness come much more from *giving* and *serving* than from *getting*.

The apostle Paul reminded his listeners that Jesus Christ had taught this very thing: "There is more happiness in *giving* than in receiving." In Acts 20:35, we read:

I have showed you all things, how that so laboring ye ought to support the weak, and to remember the words of the Lord Jesus, how he said, It is more blessed to give than to receive.

To grow in joy, we must resist not only self-pity but also self-centeredness and self-absorption. For joy to flourish, we must focus on loving others and especially on loving God.

Joy is largely composed of *gratitude* —gratitude for the wonderful things God *has done* for us and His "exceedingly great and precious *promises"* for our future.

Whereby are given unto us exceeding great and precious promises: that by these ye might be partakers of the divine nature, having escaped the corruption that is in the world through lust. (2 Peter 1:4)

Gratitude produces joy. 1 Thessalonians 5:16-18 says:

Rejoice evermore. Pray without ceasing. In everything give thanks: for this is the will of God in Christ Jesus concerning you.

And our gratitude should be for other people's blessings as well as for our own.

Rejoice with them that do rejoice, and weep with them that weep. (Romans 12:15)

Try to follow this biblical formula: Add to your life Gratitude, humility, Forgiveness, Faith, Hope, Patience and Love. Take away Resentment, Anger, Fear, Worry, Materialism, Greed, Jealousy, Complaining and Pride. The result? Joy.

3. Peace

There are many definitions we can give peace. These include: freedom from war, harmony, concord, agreement, calm, tranquility, serenity, quiet, undisturbed state of mind, absence of mental conflict, contentment, acceptance of one's state and the absence of anxiety.

The New Testament Greek word most often translated to the word "peace" is "*eirene.*" It has the sense of "joining what had previously been separated or disturbed." Thus, it is frequently used to signify "setting at one, quietness and rest." Peace is not just freedom from trouble but everything that makes for a man's highest good.

A verse in the book of Leviticus shows that God is the ultimate source of peace and He will give it upon our meeting the condition of obeying His commandments: *I will give peace in the land, and you shall lie down, and none will make you afraid; I will rid the land of evil beasts, and the sword will not go through your land.* (Leviticus 26:6)

Here, peace is a quality of life God gives even as He gives rain in due season. Leviticus 26 emphasizes material prosperity as God's blessing to Israel. Peace is necessary for the material prosperity of a nation. War may be the ultimate distraction from accomplishing anything positive; it is catastrophically debilitating to every area of life. Not only can it break a nation economically, but also warp its people psychologically and destroy its social structure, infrastructure and spirit.

Like all the fruit of the Spirit, peace is cultivated or developed as Christians mature in their spiritual walk. Peace is the absence of conflict, a state of untroubled, undisturbed believing. The Christian is to learn to walk by faith in God (believing) and not only by what appears obvious. The information in the world is not always reliable, but God's Word is truth, and therefore constantly accurate. Believing the Word of God produces peace (Romans 15:13), whereas entertaining doubts and fears results in unbelief and causes mental turmoil.

God's Word is absolute and always comes to pass. It is trustworthy and reliable. This gives the believer rock-solid confidence, and therefore strength. Strength and peace go hand in hand.

The Lord will give strength to His people; the Lord will bless His people with peace. (Psalm 29:11)

What did Jesus say about peace?

In the gospels, Jesus did not make many direct statements about peace, but one given on the eve of His crucifixion is very revealing.

Peace I leave with you, My peace I give to you; not as the world gives do I give to you. Let not your heart be troubled, neither let it be afraid. (John 14:27)

His use of the word "heart" reveals that the peace Jesus is referring to while we are in this world is a state of mind. This is confirmed in this verse: *These things I have spoken to you, that in Me you may have peace. In the world you will have tribulation; but be of good cheer, I have overcome the world.* (John 16:33)

How glorious it would be to be free of the burdens of living in this dangerous, unstable, violent world, but as sons of God such is not our lot in life. God has called us to a life that runs counter to much of this world's practices and attitudes.

As such, we are caught not only in general events and circumstances generated in the world, but also when we directly irritate and anger those close to us by determinedly following God's way. Jesus states in

His prayer to the Father in John 17:11, "*Now I am no longer in the world, but these are in the world.*"

So we become caught in and must endure this world's wars, economic swings, prejudices, social unrest, natural disasters and accidents. We are exposed to the same diseases as everybody else. All these can and do strike us with fear and trouble our hearts, destroying peace. In this world it is very easy to anticipate that a disaster can occur at any moment and therefore live in constant fear.

In John 17:14, Jesus addresses the source of the more personal persecutions that threaten our peace: "*I have given them Your word; and the world has hated them because they are not of the world, just as I am not of the world.*"

The carnal mind is enmity against God (Romans 8:7), and we can feel this hatred to a potentially terrifying degree when it is aimed directly at us. Throughout history, this sort of peace-shattering disturbance has produced job losses, divided families, uprooted lives due to fleeing, imprisonment for those caught (Acts 9:1-2; 12:3-4) and for some, martyrdom.

And yet, Jesus could sleep through a storm, totally trusting in God. Peace is a calm state of mind, resting in God's care, not being upset by the chaos of the world. Jesus acknowledged that the world offers no real peace because the god of this world, Satan, rules it. Only an intimate relationship with the Lord Jesus Christ can bring real peace.

Peace I leave with you, My peace I give to you; not as the world gives do I give to you. Let not your heart be troubled, neither let it be afraid. (John 14:27)

Colossians 3:15 says, "*Let the peace of God rule in your hearts.*"

This state of tranquility should be the norm for a believer walking by the Spirit, and any turbulence should be cause for alarm and attention.

For God is not the author of confusion but of peace, as in all the churches of the saints. (1 Corinthians 14:33)

It is essential to stay focused on God and the truth of His Word, trusting Him.

You will keep him in perfect peace, whose mind is stayed on You, because he trusts in You. (Isaiah 26:3)

Awareness of God's presence and living with God's power gives confidence, and therefore peace. God's peace transcends earthly matters, as Philippians 4:4-7 illustrates. Believers are to be "anxious for nothing," for God promises to "guard your hearts and minds." It is a peace "which transcends all understanding," that is, to the worldly mind, such peace is incomprehensible. Its source is the Holy Spirit of God, whom the world neither sees nor knows.

The Spirit of truth, whom the world cannot receive, because it neither sees Him nor knows Him; but you know Him, for He dwells with you and will be in you. (John 14:17)

The Spirit-filled Christian has a peace that is abundant, available in every situation, and unlike anything that the world has to offer (John 14:27). The alternative to being filled with the Spirit and His peace is to be filled with alarm, filled with doubt, filled with foreboding, or filled with dread. How much better to let the Spirit have control and perform His work so you can produce fruit to the glory of God!

4. Longsuffering

This is the fourth manifestation of the fruit of the spirit and to give context to explaining longsuffering, here are two scriptures that will provide a scriptural foundation:

Forbearing one another, and forgiving one another, if any man have a quarrel against any: even as Christ forgave you, so also do ye. (Colossians 3:13)

Thou therefore, my son, be strong in the grace that is in Christ Jesus. And the things that thou hast heard of me among many witnesses, the same commit thou to faithful men, who shall be able to teach others also. Thou therefore endure hardness, as a good soldier of Jesus Christ. No man that warreth entangleth himself with the affairs of this life; that he may please him who hath chosen him to be a soldier. (2 Timothy 2:1-4)

What is longsuffering?

The dictionary defines longsuffering as long and patient endurance of injury, trouble, or provocation.

Longsuffering is that quality of self-restraint in the face of provocation which does not hastily retaliate or promptly punish, it is the opposite of anger, and is associated with mercy. (Webster's)

Synonyms include forbearing, long-suffering, tolerant and uncomplaining.

Longsuffering is *love on trial*. It enables you to forbear and forgive others. As with the other manifestations of spiritual fruit, you cannot produce it in yourself. The ability to be longsuffering comes from the Holy

Spirit (Colossians 1:11) and by loving God's law (Psalm 119:165).

But let patience have her perfect work, that ye may be perfect and entire, wanting (lacking) nothing. (James 1:4)

Reaching this point is definitely a process that takes a lot of practice. However, we can learn to enjoy life where we are while we are waiting for what we desire.

Facts about longsuffering

1. It is a major attribute of God.

No greater demonstration of longsuffering can be found than that shown by God toward man. But we must understand that His longsuffering has a limit. Consider the flood, Sodom and Gomorrah, the Jews' rebellion in the wilderness, the Babylonian captivity. It is difficult to understand how God has tolerated the foolishness and the utter nonsense of the human race since the beginning of time: rebellion, idolatry, immorality, cruelty, etc.

2. Longsuffering is required of all Christians.

Ephesians 4:2 says *"With all lowliness and meekness, with longsuffering, forbearing one another in love."*

In Colossians 1:11, we read *"Strengthened with all might, according to his glorious power, unto all patience and longsuffering with joyfulness."*

Colossians 3:12 also says *"Put on therefore, as the elect of God, holy and beloved, bowels of mercies, kindness, humbleness of mind, meekness, longsuffering."*

The opposite of longsuffering is short-temperedness. God

expects us to control our temper. While all Christians are to be longsuffering, it develops to higher degrees as one matures in age and knowledge.

Short-temperedness can make one lose the promise as explained in Hebrews 10:36 *"For ye have need of patience, that, after ye have done the will of God, ye might receive the promise"*.

Longsuffering is necessary to be able to get along where there are differences on many subjects. It is easy for those who are mature to be impatient toward those who are less mature. It may have taken them years to come to their present level of knowledge, but the mature are often not willing to give the immature the same amount of time and study to reach their level of knowledge and understanding. This act is manifestly unfair, and lacking in longsuffering. Paul said, *"Him that is weak in the faith receive ye, but not to doubtful disputations."* (Romans 14:1) and *"We then that are strong ought to bear the infirmities of the weak, and not to please ourselves."* (Romans 15:1)

3. It can be exhausted.

The longsuffering of God was in effect in the days of Noah while the ark was being prepared, but the time came when the attitude of the people exhausted the longsuffering of God and He destroyed the earth by the flood. In Genesis 6:3 the Bible says *"And the Lord said, My spirit shall not always strive with man, for that he also is flesh: yet his days shall be an hundred and twenty years."* God is said to be longsuffering to us, but it is not inexhaustible. He is not willing that any should perish, but that all should come to repentance (2 Peter 3:9), but His longsuffering does not outreach man's wickedness and stubbornness.

How do I develop the fruit of longsuffering?

· You must be persistent to develop it. It does not come by accident.

· Start with yourself. If we are impatient with ourselves, it will be impossible to manifest longsuffering toward others. This is a common failure. We are impatient with our own shortcomings and mistakes. We get angry toward ourselves when things go wrong. This happens more frequently as we grow older, and our minds cease to be as sharp as they once were. We become frustrated at our own absentmindedness.

· Realize that the development of longsuffering is strictly your responsibility. If you do not have it, you cannot shift the reason for the lack of it to someone else. Every man is the sole proprietor of his own physical mind and body. Paul makes this clear in 1 Corinthians 9:27. Peter admonishes the individual Christian to add it to his faith (2 Peter 1:5-11).

But I keep under my body, and bring it into subjection: lest that by any means, when I have preached to others, I myself should be a castaway. (1 Corinthians 9:27)

· Following the "golden rule" found in Matthew 7 verse 12 is required for the development of longsuffering that is, be as patient with others as you want others to be with you.

Therefore, whatever you want men to do to you, do also to them, for this is the Law and the Prophets. (Matthew 7:12)

· Study Gods word diligently. This will impress upon you how important longsuffering is in living an overcoming life. Through the scriptures, you will observe this quality in God, Christ, the Holy Spirit, Paul and other Christians who exemplified longsuffering to a high degree.

...whose faiths follow, considering the end of their conversation. (Hebrews 13:7)

At this point, I want you to consider the uselessness and possible harm that can be done through impatience. The things we say and do out of a lack of longsuffering are seldom good or a source of personal satisfaction. In fact we often need to apologize for the things we say and do out of impatience. Personal satisfaction usually comes from realizing that we did the wise thing by restraining our words and actions in situations where we might have acted otherwise.

5. Gentleness

Gentleness simply refers to "true humility that does not consider itself too good or too exalted for humble tasks". It is a polite, restrained behavior toward others. Every person is powerful. We can speak words that influence others; we can act in ways that help or hurt; and we can choose what influences others through our words and actions. Gentleness constrains and channels that power.

Gentleness also means giving up the right to judge what is best for others and yourself. The truth is God is not as concerned with our comfort as with our spiritual growth, and He knows how to help us grow far better than we do. By accepting and recognizing that God's ways and thoughts are higher than ours, we can begin to exhibit a gentle and calm demeanor to the matters of life. Gentleness means that we accept that the rain falls on the evil and the just and that God may use methods we don't like to reach our hearts and the hearts of others.

Gentleness is a deliberate refusal to use your power or influence to harm anyone, an unwillingness to 'cut and slash' at people, deliberately wounding them for the sake of taking vengeance, spite or control. Gentleness desires that no harm be done to others. A gentle person does not seek to make other people angry. Gentleness may mean you lose certain battles, but it certainly helps win the overall struggle. A person of gentle response tends to create fewer enemies, and more friends.

Gentleness is a strong hand with a soft touch. It is a tender, compassionate approach toward others' weaknesses and limitations. A gentle person still speaks the truth, even painful truth sometimes, but in doing so guards his tone so the truth can be well received.

Gentleness is a thing of the heart. That is why Jesus said in Matthew 11:29 *"I am gentle and humble in heart."*

6. Goodness

Goodness refers to something that meets a certain standard or someone's expectations. It fulfills the goal of the job. Goodness, or the idea of being good, means that the thing fulfills its purpose or the expectations for it. **There is no way we can talk about goodness without God.** True goodness can only flow out of a life that is right with God and yielded to Him. Micah 7:2 says *"The good man is perished out of the earth: and there is none upright among men: they all lie in wait for blood; they hunt every man his brother with a net."*

Man in his natural state cannot do any good and this is why we must rely on the help of the Holy Spirit. Paul captures this truth succinctly in Romans 7:14-25:

For we know that the law is spiritual: but I am carnal, sold under sin.

For that which I do I allow not: for what I would, that do I not; but what I hate, that do I.

If then I do that which I would not; I consent unto the law that it is good.

Now then it is no more I that do it, but sin that dwelleth in me.

For I know that in me (that is, in my flesh,) dwelleth no good thing: for to will is present with me; but how to perform that which is good I find not.

For the good that I would I do not: but the evil which I would not, that I do.

Now if I do that I would not, it is no more I that do it, but sin that dwelleth in me.

I find then a law, that, when I would do good, evil is present with me.

For I delight in the law of God after the inward man:

But I see another law in my members, warring against the law of my mind, and bringing me into captivity to the law of sin which is in my members.

O wretched man that I am! who shall deliver me from the body of this death?

I thank God through Jesus Christ our Lord. So then with the mind I myself serve the law of God; but with the flesh the law of sin.

What is Jesus view about goodness?

One of the most famous and interesting passages in the Bible is Luke 18:18, 19 which details an encounter between a rich young ruler and Jesus. The rich young ruler calls Jesus good Teacher, or Master in some versions. "*Why do you call me good?*" Jesus answered, "*No one is good, except God alone*" (NIV).

What a fascinating response from Jesus. We can talk about good people and good things in terms of human standards and our expectations for them; but when it really comes down to it, who sets the ultimate standard and expectations for goodness except God? Jesus was challenging the young ruler to consider the truth that He was God come in the flesh and that appreciating God's holiness and the gift of

His Son would end the thinking that there is anything one can do to earn salvation. Thirdly, John 11-12 says *"Beloved, follow not that which is evil, but that which is good. He that doeth good is of God: but he that doeth evil hath not seen God. Demetrius hath good report of all men, and of the truth itself: yea, and we also bear record; and ye know that our record is true."*

Can any man meet God's standard of goodness? One of the very few people that the Bible refers to as being good, was a man called Barnabas. His story can be found in two places in the book of Acts. The first is in Acts 4:33-37 where the Bible says *"And with great power gave the apostles witness of the resurrection of the Lord Jesus: and great grace was upon them all. Neither was there any among them that lacked: for as many as were possessors of lands or houses sold them, and brought the prices of the things that were sold, and laid them down at the apostles' feet: and distribution was made unto every man according as he had need.*

And Joses, who by the apostles was surnamed Barnabas, (which is, being interpreted, The son of consolation,) a Levite, and of the country of Cyprus, having land, sold it, and brought the money, and laid it at the apostles' feet."

In Acts 11:19-26, the Bible also says *"Now they which were scattered abroad upon the persecution that arose about Stephen travelled as far as Phenice, and Cyprus, and Antioch, preaching the word to none but unto the Jews only.*

And some of them were men of Cyprus and Cyrene, which, when they were come to Antioch, spake unto the Grecians, preaching the Lord Jesus.

And the hand of the Lord was with them: and a great number believed, and turned unto the Lord. Then tidings of these things came unto the ears of the church which was in Jerusalem: and they sent forth Barnabas, that he should go as far as Antioch. Who, when he came, and had seen the grace of God, was glad, and exhorted them all, that with purpose of heart they would cleave unto the Lord.

For he was a good man, and full of the Holy Ghost and of faith: and much people was added unto the Lord. Then departed Barnabas to Tarsus, for to seek Saul: And when he had found him, he brought him unto Antioch. And it came to pass, that a whole year they assembled themselves with the church, and taught much people. And the disciples were called Christians first in Antioch."

From the above scriptures, four main attributes made Barnabas qualify for the title "good."

1. He was generous and selfless. *Acts 4:37*

2. He was full of the Holy Ghost. *Acts 11:24*

3. He was full of faith. *Acts 11:24*

4. He was diligent. *Acts 11:22-26*

There are four attributes that God looks for before He can see you as being good:

1. God must direct all his ways. Psalm 37:23 says *"The steps of a good man are ordered by the Lord: and he delighteth in his way."*

2. He must be generous and wise. Psalm 112:5 says *"A good man sheweth favor, and lendeth: he will guide his affairs with discretion."*

3. A good man must fully provide for his family and even generations unborn. Proverbs 13:22 says *"A good man leaveth an inheritance to his children's children: and the wealth of the sinner is laid up for the just."*

4. A good man will always produce good things. Luke 6:45 says *"A good man out of the good treasure of his heart bringeth forth that which is good; and an evil man out of the evil treasure of his heart*

bringeth forth that which is evil: for of the abundance of the heart his mouth speaketh."

In conclusion, the presence of the Holy Spirit in our lives activates the divine ability to produce goodness. The Holy Spirit anoints and empowers you to *do good.* Acts 10:38 says *"How God anointed Jesus of Nazareth with the Holy Ghost and with power: who went about doing good, and healing all that were oppressed of the devil; for God was with him."*

7. Faith

Faith is a gift and also a manifestation of the fruit of the Spirit. The gift of faith is imparted from God through the Word, but the Holy Spirit produces the fruit of faith. The gift of faith can move mountains, but the fruit of faith is what is required for daily living. The fruit of faith enables us to walk and live by faith (Romans 5:2). Without this kind of faith, it is impossible to please

Hebrews 11:6 says *"Without **faith** it is impossible to please him, for he that cometh to God must believe that He is, and that He is a rewarder of them that diligently seek Him."* (Emphasis Mine)

Matthew 17:20 says *"If ye have **faith** as a grain of mustard seed, ye shall say unto this mountain, 'Remove hence to yonder place;' and it shall remove; and nothing shall be impossible unto you."* (Emphasis Mine)

Matthew 21:22 says *"And all things, whatsoever ye shall ask in prayer, believing, ye shall receive."*

Mark 11:24 says *"Therefore I say unto you, what things whatsoever ye desire, when ye pray, believe that ye receive them, and ye shall have them."*

Abraham was a classic example of the fruit of faith. Romans 4:17-25 says, *"(As it is written, I have made thee a father of many nations,) before him whom he believed, even God, who quickeneth the dead, and calleth those things which be not as though they were. Who against hope believed in hope, that he might become the father of many nations; according to that which was spoken, So shall thy seed be. And being not weak in faith, he considered not his own body now dead, when he was about an hundred years old, neither yet the deadness of Sara's womb: He staggered not at the promise of God through unbelief; but was strong in faith, giving glory to God; and being fully persuaded that, what he had promised, he was able also to perform. And therefore it was imputed to him for righteousness. Now it was not written for his sake alone, that it was imputed to him; But for us also, to whom it shall be imputed, if we believe on him that raised up Jesus our Lord from the dead; Who was delivered for our offences, and was raised again for our justification."*

The source of faith

Romans 10:17 says *"So then faith cometh by hearing, and hearing by the word of God."*

Faith as a fruit of the Spirit starts as a seed, which can only grow by the water of the Word. The Word of God must abide in you in order for your faith to grow and for you to become immovable.

John 15:5-7 also says *"I am the vine, ye are the branches: He that abideth in me, and I in him, the same bringeth forth much fruit: for without me ye can do nothing.*

If a man abide not in me, he is cast forth as a branch, and is withered; and men gather them, and cast them into the fire, and they are burned.

If ye abide in me, and my words abide in you, ye shall ask what ye will, and it shall be done unto you."

Faith in action

Two stories, one in the Old Testament and the other in the New Testament will clearly explain faith as a fruit of the Spirit.

1. Abraham and God

Hebrews 11:8-10 captures the personality and character of Abraham subtly thus: *"By faith Abraham, when he was called to go out into a place which he should after receive for an inheritance, obeyed; and he went out, not knowing whither he went. By faith he sojourned in the land of promise, as in a strange country, dwelling in tabernacles with Isaac and Jacob, the heirs with him of the same promise: For he looked for a city which hath foundations, whose builder and maker is God."*

Verses 17-19 continues:
"By faith Abraham, when he was tried, offered up Isaac: and he that had received the promises offered up his only begotten son, Of whom it was said, That in Isaac shall thy seed be called: Accounting that God was able to raise him up, even from the dead; from whence also he received him in a figure."

The story of Abraham as a father of faith can be broken into blocks:

a. Abram received a promise from God.

> *After these things the word of the Lord came unto Abram in a vision, saying, Fear not, Abram: I am thy shield, and thy exceeding great reward. And Abram said, Lord God, what wilt thou give me, seeing I go childless, and the steward of my house is this Eliezer of Damascus?*
> *And Abram said, Behold, to me thou hast given no seed: and, lo, one born in my house is mine heir. And, behold, the word of the Lord came unto him, saying, This shall not be thine heir; but he that shall come forth out of thine*

own bowels shall be thine heir.

And he brought him forth abroad, and said, Look now toward heaven, and tell the stars, if thou be able to number them: and he said unto him, So shall thy seed be. And he believed in the Lord; and he counted it to him for righteousness. And he said unto him, I am the Lord that brought thee out of Ur of the Chaldees, to give thee this land to inherit it.
(Genesis 15:1-7)

b. Abraham submitted to Sarah's desire for an alternative.

Now Sarai Abram's wife bare him no children: and she had an handmaid, an Egyptian, whose name was Hagar. And Sarai said unto Abram, Behold now, the Lord hath restrained me from bearing: I pray thee, go in unto my maid; it may be that I may obtain children by her. And Abram hearkened to the voice of Sarai.And Sarai Abram's wife took Hagar her maid the Egyptian, after Abram had dwelt ten years in the land of Canaan, and gave her to her husband Abram to be his wife. And he went in unto Hagar, and she conceived: and when she saw that she had conceived, her mistress was despised in her eyes.

And Sarai said unto Abram, My wrong be upon thee: I have given my maid into thy bosom; and when she saw that she had conceived, I was despised in her eyes: the Lord judge between me and thee. But Abram said unto Sarai, Behold, thy maid is in thy hand; do to her as it pleaseth thee. And when Sarai dealt hardly with her, she fled from her face. And the angel of the Lord found her by a fountain of water in the wilderness, by the fountain in the way to Shur.

And he said, Hagar, Sarai's maid, whence camest thou? and whither wilt thou go? And she said, I flee from the face of my mistress Sarai. And the angels of the Lord said unto her, Return to thy mistress, and submit thyself under her hands. And the angel of the Lord said unto her, I will multiply thy seed exceedingly, that it shall not be numbered for multitude. And the angel of the Lord said unto her, Behold, thou art with child, and shalt bear a son, and shalt call his name Ishmael; because the Lord hath heard thy affliction. And he will be a wild man; his hand will be against every man, and every man's hand against him; and he shall dwell in the presence of all his brethren.

(Genesis 16:1-12)

c. God gave Abraham a child of promise in his old age

And the Lord visited Sarah as he had said, and the Lord did unto Sarah as he had spoken. For Sarah conceived, and bare Abraham a son in his old age, at the set time of which God had spoken to him.

And Abraham called the name of his son that was born unto him, whom Sarah bare to him, Isaac. And Abraham circumcised his son Isaac being eight days old, as God had commanded him. And Abraham was an hundred years old, when his son Isaac was born unto him.

And Sarah said, God hath made me to laugh, so that all that hear will laugh with me.

And she said, Who would have said unto Abraham, that Sarah should have given children suck? for I have born him a son in his old age.

(Genesis 21:1-7)

d. Abraham passed the greatest test of faith

And it came to pass after these things that God did tempt Abraham, and said unto him, Abraham: and he said, Behold, here I am.
And he said, Take now thy son, thine only son Isaac, whom thou lovest, and get thee into the land of Moriah; and offer him there for a burnt offering upon one of the mountains which I will tell thee of.

And Abraham rose up early in the morning, and saddled his ass, and took two of his young men with him, and Isaac his son, and clave the wood for the burnt offering, and rose up, and went unto the place of which God had told him.

Then on the third day Abraham lifted up his eyes, and saw the place afar off. And Abraham said unto his young men, Abide ye here with the ass; and I and the lad will go yonder and worship, and come again to you.

And Abraham took the wood of the burnt offering, and laid it upon Isaac his son; and he took the fire in his hand, and a knife; and they went both of them together.

And Isaac spake unto Abraham his father, and said, My father: and he said, Here am I, my son. And he said, Behold the fire and the wood: but where is the lamb for a burnt offering?

And Abraham said, My son, God will provide himself a lamb for a burnt offering: so they went both of them together. And they came to the place which God had told him of; and Abraham built an altar there, and laid the wood in order, and bound Isaac his son, and laid him on the altar upon the wood. And Abraham stretched forth his hand, and took the knife to slay his son.

And the angel of the Lord called unto him out of heaven, and said, Abraham, Abraham: and he said, Here am I. And he said, Lay not thine hand upon the lad, neither do thou any thing unto him: for now I know that thou fearest God, seeing thou hast not withheld thy son, thine only son from me.

And Abraham lifted up his eyes, and looked, and behold behind him a ram caught in a thicket by his horns: and Abraham went and took the ram, and offered him up for a burnt offering in the stead of his son.

And Abraham called the name of that place Jehovah–jireh: as it is said to this day, In the mount of the Lord it shall be seen. Jehovah–jireh: that is, The Lord will see, or, provide.

And the angel of the Lord called unto Abraham out of heaven the second time,

And said, By myself have I sworn, saith the Lord, for because thou hast done this thing, and hast not withheld thy son, thine only son:

That in blessing I will bless thee, and in multiplying I will multiply thy seed as the stars of the heaven, and as the sand which is upon the sea shore; and thy seed shall possess the gate of his

And in thy seed shall all the nations of the earth be blessed; because thou hast obeyed my voice. So Abraham returned unto his young men, and they rose up and went together to Beer–sheba; and Abraham dwelt at Beer–sheba.
(Genesis 22:1-19)

2. The Centurion and Jesus

There is a wonderful picture of faith in action in Matthew 8:5-10, 13.

"And when Jesus was entered into Capernaum, there came unto him a centurion, beseeching him, And saying, Lord, my servant lieth at home sick of the palsy, grievously tormented. And Jesus saith unto him, I will come and heal him. The centurion answered and said, Lord, I am not worthy that thou shouldest come under my roof: but speak the word only, and my servant shall be healed. For I am a man under authority, having soldiers under me: and I say to this man, Go, and he goeth; and to another, Come, and he cometh; and to my servant, Do this, and he doeth it. When Jesus heard it, he marvelled, and said to them that followed, Verily I say unto you, I have not found so great faith, no, not in Israel. ... And Jesus said unto the centurion, Go thy way; and as thou hast believed, so be it done unto thee. And his servant was healed in the selfsame hour."

What a beautiful picture of trusting faith! I do not know about you, but I had to stop and meditate when I read this story. How strong is your faith? Is it even as big as the grain of a mustard seed? God can use you mightily if you will simply believe in Him.

"Expect great things from God, attempt great things for God."
- William Carey

In conclusion, Habakkuk 2:4b says, *"but the just shall live by his faith."* The Christian life cannot be lived without faith. Faith as a fruit of the Spirit must be continually watered by the Word and built experientially by acting on the Word. The more of tshe Word you do, the more God delivers and the more God delivers, the more you want to put your trust in Him to do more. This is how 1 Corinthians 15:58 that says *"Therefore, my beloved brethren, be ye steadfast, unmovable, always abounding in the work of the Lord, forasmuch as ye know that your labor is not in vain in the Lord"* can be fulfilled in our lives.

8. Meekness

Let this mind be in you which was also in Christ Jesus, who, being in the form of God, did not consider it robbery to be equal with God, but made Himself of no reputation, taking the form of a bondservant, and coming in the likeness of men. And being found in appearance as a man, He humbled Himself and became obedient to the point of death, even the death of the cross. Therefore God also has highly exalted Him and given Him the name which is above every name, that at the name of Jesus every knee should bow, of those in heaven, and of those on earth, and of those under the earth, and that every tongue should confess that Jesus Christ is Lord, to the glory of God the Father. (Philippians 2:4-11)

Meekness is an attitude or quality of heart whereby a person willingly accepts and submits without resistance to the will and desires of someone else. The meek person is not continually concerned with self, personal ways, ideas or wishes. He is willing to put himself in second place and submit himself to achieve what is good for others.

Meekness is the opposite of self-will, self-interest, and self-assertiveness. This is a sign, not of weakness of character (as some think), but of strength. It requires great self-control to submit to others.

The meek are those who quietly submit themselves to God, to His word and to His correction, who follow His directions and comply with His designs, and are gentle towards all men. Meekness enables a person to bear patiently those insults and injuries he receives at the hand of others. It makes him ready to accept instruction from the least of the saints. It allows him to endure provocation without being inflamed by it. He remains cool when others become heated.

Meek people seek no private revenge; they leave that to God's sense of justice while they seek to remain true in their calling and meet God's standards. The meek is satisfied with what he has. Contentment of mind is one of the manifestations of meekness. The haughty and covetous do not inherit the earth.

Godly meekness is impossible unless we first accept a just and lowly estimate of ourselves. We do this by coming before God in deep penitence and with a clear knowledge of the vast difference between ourselves and what He is and what He means us to be. Paul says in Romans 12:3, *"For I say, through the grace given to me, to everyone who is among you, not to think of himself more highly than he ought to think, but to think soberly, as God has dealt to each one a measure of faith."* While pride destroys self and others, humility serves and builds.

Jesus our example in meekness

The supreme example of meekness is Jesus Christ, who endured horrific trials. John 18:11 says, *"Then Jesus said to Peter, 'Put your sword into the sheath. Shall I not drink the cup which My Father has given Me?"* Acts 8:32 provides more insight on Christ's meek reaction: *"He was led (not dragged) as a sheep to the slaughter; and like a lamb silent before its shearer, so He opened not His mouth."* He was the very King of meekness. Meekness is so important that it is the third characteristic Jesus mentions in His foundational teaching known as the Sermon on the Mount: *"Blessed are the meek, for they shall inherit the earth."* (Matthew 5:5).

In Matthew 11:29, Jesus explains why we should embrace His way of life. As our Lord and Master, He is not harsh, overbearing and oppressive, but gentle in His government. His laws are also reasonable and easy to obey and does not enslave. Jesus emphasizes the gentle aspect of meekness toward others. From this, we begin to see why meekness must be a virtue of those who will receive the Kingdom and govern. Because God governs in meekness, His children must also.

A meek person will feel the wrong done against him and though hurt bitterly, does not allow his spirit to give way to a hateful, savage and vindictive anger that seeks to "get even." He will instead be full of pity for the damaged character, attitudes and blindness of the perpetrator. From the cross Jesus uttered, *"Father, forgive them, for they do not know what they do"* (Luke 23:34). This virtue is a strong bulwark against self-righteousness, intolerance and the critical judgment of others.

Benefits of meekness

- ### Satisfaction and contentment

The meek shall eat and be satisfied: they shall praise the Lord that seek him: your heart shall live for ever. (Psalm 22:26)

- **Divine Promotion**

The Lord lifteth up the meek: he casteth the wicked down to the ground. (Psalm 147:6)

- **Divine Joy**

The meek also shall increase their joy in the Lord, and the poor among men shall rejoice in the Holy One of Israel. (Isaiah 29:19)

9. Temperance

Temperance is defined as "moderation in action, thought, or feeling; restraint or self-control." Temperance means the abstinence from all that is evil, and the moderate use of all that is good. Temperance is the ability to govern oneself completely in all circumstances of life. Temperance is the virtue that applies to times of ease and times of crisis; times of wealth and times of poverty; times of health and times of sickness; times when one is full of ambitious energy and times when at the end of the day one is thoroughly drained.

Temperance in these situations means to have spiritual control over ourselves so that we continue in the life of godliness, love, and thankfulness to our heavenly Father. It means we are to weigh what is best and abstain from the rest. It helps us know how to sacrifice the lesser for the higher good, how to discern between the good and the best. That is the sign of spiritual maturity. Hebrews 12:1 says *"Wherefore seeing we also are compassed about with so great a cloud of witnesses, let us lay aside every weight, and the sin which doth so easily beset us, and let us run with patience the race that is set before us".*

What is a weight? It is anything in life that keeps us from being our best for God. So a weight maybe something easily justified as right and good in the sense that it is not outright sin but it may keep us from winning the Christian race. Self-control requires us not only to avoid sin but also demands the discipline to give up good things that will keep us from being and doing our best for God.

Self-control means moderation and restraint in the things that are legitimate and the elimination of those things that tear down or destroy your spiritual life. This virtue applies to so many things in our lives, including the use of our time. Are you temperate or disciplined with your use of the gift of time? Do you make time for significant prayer each day with God? Do you take time to study and meditate on the Scriptures? Temperance also applies to what you eat. Are you temperate with your food, eating in moderation?

Jesus, our example in temperance

Then was Jesus led up of the Spirit into the wilderness to be tempted of the devil. And when he had fasted forty days and forty nights, he was afterward an hungred. And when the tempter came to him, he said, If thou be the Son of God, command that these stones be made bread. But he answered and said, It is written, Man shall not live by bread alone, but by every word that proceedeth out of the mouth of God. Then the devil taketh him up into the holy city, and setteth him on a pinnacle of the temple, and saith unto him, If thou be the Son of God, cast thyself down: for it is written, He shall give his angels charge concerning thee: and in their hands they shall bear thee up, lest at any time thou dash thy foot against a stone. Jesus said unto him, It is written again, Thou shalt not tempt the Lord thy God. Again, the devil taketh him up into an exceeding high mountain, and sheweth him all the kingdoms of the world, and the glory of them; And saith unto him, All these things will I give thee, if thou wilt fall down and worship me. Then saith Jesus unto him, Get thee hence, Satan: for it is written, Thou shalt worship the Lord thy God, and him only shalt thou serve. Then the devil leaveth him, and, behold, angels came and ministered unto him. (Matthew 4:1-11)

In the above scripture we see Jesus facing Satan's temptation after a long fast that lasted for forty days and forty nights. His body was weak and the devil tempted him with food but Jesus responded in verse 4: *"But he answered and said, It is written, Man shall not live by bread alone, but by every word that proceedeth out of the mouth of God.* Here we can see temperance is the willingness and ability to say no even to our most urgent desires. Jesus Christ exercised control over his flesh.

In verses 5 - 6, Satan tempted Jesus' soul with pride and He resisted this temptation by replying in verse 7 *"It is written again, Thou shalt not tempt the Lord thy God"*.

In verses 8 and 9, Satan tempted Jesus spiritually by encouraging Him to worship him. But Jesus replied him by saying in verse 10 *"Get thee hence, Satan: for it is written, Thou shalt worship the Lord thy God, and him only shalt thou serve"*.

At the end of His ordeal, being victorious over Satan, angels came and ministered to Jesus. He won the battle by exuding temperance and self-control.

How can a believer exercise self-control?

The only way to exercise temperance in all things is to guard your thoughts and desires. You need to remember that the mind is the source, or origin of all you do and say. If I am going to control my words and actions, it must begin with my mind. Many people, today, try to make some changes in their lives or break a bad habit or even form a new one without much success. The truth is, many attempts at change are merely "superficial." This is because the change was merely an outward change without the mind of the person changing.

In such cases, we see that their change is short-lived. If there is a part of your life over which you have no control, you must begin with changing your mindset and your attitude. You must make a conscious decision to think what is right, and the body (in actions and speech) will follow. This principle is found time and time again in the Bible.

In Proverbs 4:23, Solomon said, *"Keep thy heart with all diligence; for out of it are the issues of life"*. Jesus told His disciples in Matthew 15:18-20 *"Those things which proceed out of the mouth come forth from the heart; and they defile the man. For out of the heart proceed evil thoughts, murders, adulteries, fornications, thefts, false witness, and blasphemies: These are the things which defile a man..."*

In fact, Paul wrote to the Colossians in Colossians 3:23, *"And whatsoever ye do, do it heartily, as to the Lord, and not unto men"*. The word "heartily" carries the idea of "from the heart," or soul of a man. Therefore, we must guard our hearts (minds) from things that would lend themselves to making us meditate on sinful things.

In Philippians 4:8, the Bible says *"Finally, brethren, whatsoever things are true, whatsoever things are honest, whatsoever things are just, whatsoever things are pure, whatsoever things are lovely, whatsoever things are of good report; if there be any virtue, and if there be any praise, think on these things"*.

There may be some places that you can no longer visit if you are going to have the self-control God wants you to have. The Bible tell us, *"Out of the abundance of the heart the mouth speaketh"* (Matthew 12:34). Friend, what are you putting "in your heart"? Are you "keeping" or guarding it as you should? Once I bring *"into captivity every thought to the obedience of Christ"* (2 Corinthians 10:5), then my words and actions will follow. This is the point of temperance, or self-control. I need to make sure that all that I am is under the control of Christ Jesus, the Lord. He has all authority (Matthew 28:18), and I have none. Therefore, my responsibility in life is to Him, and to control my thoughts, speech, and actions to reflect His will and not my own (Colossians 3:17).

A temperate or self-controlled person will show calmness, personal care, tenderness and the Love of Christ in meeting the needs of others. It is more than the result of a personality change; it is who we are from the work of the Spirit within us.

Chapter 3
The Works of the Flesh

In the last chapter, I explained the fruit of the Spirit but just as we have these powerful and positive spiritual attributes, there are also the works of the flesh that struggle against our spirit. To live an overcoming life, you must not only understand the fruit of the Spirit and work to ensure that you are growing in them but also have a thorough understanding of the works of the flesh. This will empower you to live a life worthy of the Kingdom of God, with great fruit and great results.

1. Idolatry
The first is Idolatry and is singularly one of the most destructive forces in the history of humanity and is still a bane to Christians today.

What is idolatry?
    1.   Worship of idols.

2. Extreme admiration, love, or reverence for something or someone.

Most people today who have any concept of idolatry probably think of pagans bowing down and worshipping a strange-looking idol - a carved image or statue. This is only a part of what idolatry means, but since most of us today do not engage in such, how do God's commands against idolatry apply to Christians now?

The opposite of worship is idolatry. Every human being - at every moment of their life, today and into eternity - is unceasingly doing either the former or the latter.

Idolatry occurs when you begin to value anything more than you value God. Idolatry is spending more time thinking about your hero more than God. If your every thought is about the latest gadget or your personal appearance, that is also idolatry. Let me shock you: If the first priority in your life is your family before God, even that is idolatry.

When God said, "*You shall have no other gods before me*" (Exodus 20:3), He was not just talking about the imaginary deities that seem so ridiculous to us today and yet certain cultures still celebrate, He was talking about anything that usurps His place as number one in our hearts.

Before God, Christians are not defined by skin color, gender, geographical location, or even, shockingly, by their good behavior. Nor are they defined by the particular type of religious feelings they may have. They are defined in terms of the 'God/god(s)' they worship. God is particular about where your heart is. In Matthew 6:21 the Bible says *"For where your treasure is, there will your heart be also"*.

WAYS TO AVOID IDOLATRY

- Be careful of turning a good thing, such as marriage, sex, children, health, success, or financial stability, an ultimate thing, or what Jesus called our "treasure" into things that come before God.

- Avoid participating in any religious community where the clear truth of the Scripture is ignored while contemplative and mystical practices are favored simply for a spiritual experience.

- Be careful not to worship a good thing as a God thing for that is a bad thing.

2. Witchcraft

You must also avoid the practice of magic, black magic, the use of spells and the invocation of spirits.

Witchcraft, also called black magic, is the use of supernatural powers sourced from the devil and his domain. Witchcraft is a religion. People who practice this religion are called "Witches." Most State Governments, the Federal Government and even the United States Armed Forces recognize the religion of Witchcraft.

Biblical Views about witchcraft

There are several scriptures that talk about witchcraft or the occult and we shall look at just two of them:

DEUTERONOMY 18:9-14

> *When thou art come into the land which the Lord thy God giveth thee, thou shalt not learn to do after the abominations of those nations.*

There shall not be found among you any one that maketh his son or his daughter to pass through the fire, or that useth divination, or an observer of times, or an enchanter, or a witch, or a charmer, or a consulter with familiar spirits, or a wizard, or a necromancer.

For all that do these things are an abomination unto the Lord: and because of these abominations the Lord thy God doth drive them out from before thee. Thou shalt be perfect with the Lord thy God.

For these nations, which thou shalt possess, hearkened unto observers of times, and unto diviners: but as for thee, the Lord thy God hath not suffered thee so to do.

LEVITICUS 19:26-28,31

You shall not eat anything with the blood, nor practice divination or soothsaying. You shall not round off the side-growth of your heads nor harm the edges of your beard.

You shall not make any cuts in your body for the dead nor make any tattoo marks on yourselves :I am the LORD.

Do not turn to mediums or spiritists; do not seek them out to be defiled by them. I am the LORD your God.

From the above two scriptures; there are nine terms that have to do with witchcraft and their definitions:

1. Casting spells: The act of charming or "tying up" a person through magic- used in the sense of binding with a charm consisting of words of occult power.

2. Divination: The act of divining sorcery, soothsaying which is a pagan contrast to true prophecy or man's attempt to know and control the world and future apart from the true God. It involves using inhuman means; foretelling or foreseeing the future or discovering hidden knowledge through reading omens, dreams, using lots, astrology, or necromancy.

3. Interpreting omens: A type of divination, seeking insight or knowledge through signs or events.

4. Medium: One who foretells events or gains information by conversing with spirits of the dead.

5. Necromancer: One who calls up the dead; also called a Medium.

6. Spiritist: A diviner or familiar spirit; one who has esoteric knowledge through non-human means.

7. Soothsaying: This refers to those who observe the clouds for augury; foretelling future events with supernatural power but not divine power; interpreting dreams and revealing secrets.

8. Sorcerer: Another word used interchangeably for magician, conjurer, enchanter, one who practices magic arts, sorcery, charms, with an intent to do harm or to delude or pervert the mind; one who claims to have supernatural power or knowledge through (evil) spirits.

9. Witchcraft: This is the practice of witches and wizards and involves the use of formulas and incantations.

The Bible makes it clear that God detests any of these acts and there were strong and grave punishments for those involved in such. Nothing good comes out of the devil and though mainstream media and Hollywood often attempts to celebrate good or white witches, any form of witchcraft is an abomination unto God. Stay away from such practices.

3. Hatred

Hatred is defined as "intense dislike" or "ill-will." Other synonyms include enmity, animosity or detestation. Hatred (or hate) is a deep and emotional extreme dislike that can be directed against individuals, entities, objects, or ideas. Hatred is often associated with feelings of anger and a disposition towards hostility. You cannot walk in the Spirit and hate your brother.

In fact, God detests hatred and there are several scriptures that talk about it:

If anyone says, "I love God," and hates his brother, he is a liar; for he who does not love his brother whom he has seen cannot love God whom he has not seen. (I John 4:20)

Whoever says he is in the light and hates his brother is still in darkness. (I John 2:9)

Hatred stirs up strife, but love covers all offenses. (Proverbs 10:12)

But if you do not forgive others their trespasses, neither will your Father forgive your trespasses. (Matthew 6:15)

But I say to you, Love your enemies and pray for those who persecute you. (Matthew 5:44)

But whoever hates his brother is in the darkness and walks in the darkness, and does not know where he is going, because the darkness has blinded his eyes. (I John 2:11)

A classical biblical demonstration of the sin of hatred can be found in the book of Genesis 4:1-10 when Cain killed his brother Abel.

4. Variance

Variance refers to a lifestyle of constant disagreement or quarrelling or discord. It refers to a difference that produces dispute or controversy, disagreement, dissension or discord. Uncontrolled variance can lead to enmity. It also refers to unnecessary and prolonged debate, wrangling and contention.

As children of God, God expects us to be sober.

1 Peter 5:8 says, *"Be sober, be vigilant; because your adversary the devil, as a roaring lion, walketh about, and seeking whom he may devour."*

Ecclesiastes 9:17 says, *"The words of wise men are heard in quiet more than the cry of him that ruleth among fools."*

Isaiah 30:15 says, *"For thus saith the Lord God, the Holy One of Israel; In returning and rest shall ye be saved; in quietness and in confidence shall be your strength: and ye would not."*

2 Timothy 2:16 says, *"But shun profane and vain babblings: for they will increase unto more ungodliness."*

1 Timothy 6:20 says, *"O Timothy, keep that which is committed to thy trust, avoiding profane and vain babblings, and oppositions of science falsely so called."*

5. Emulations

Another work of the flesh is Emulation. What is emulation? Emulation means striving to equal or excel in qualities or actions with another person; to imitate, with a view to equal or excel; to vie with or to rival. It signifies the stirring up of jealousy or envy in others, because of what we are, or have, or profess.

Emulation refers to the spirit of competition where men want to outdo one another.

The Bible says in James 3:16 that *"For where envying and strife is, there is confusion and every evil work."* In other words where envying and strife are, there is confusion. Everything is unsettled and agitated. There is no mutual confidence and there is definitely no unity of purpose and effort. There is no co-operation in promoting a common object nor is there stability in the pursuit or execution of any plan. Even when there is a good purpose formed by one party, it is willfully defeated by the other person.

The spirit of God does not thrive in an atmosphere of competition.

In 1 Corinthians 3:1-3, the Bible says *"However, brethren, I could not talk to you as to spiritual (men), but as to nonspiritual (men of the flesh, in whom the carnal nature predominates), as to mere infants (in the new life) in Christ (unable to talk yet!) 2I fed you with milk, not solid food, for you were not yet strong enough (to be ready for it); but even yet you are not strong enough (to be ready for it), 3For you are still (unspiritual, having the nature) of the flesh (under the control of ordinary impulses). For as long as (there are) envying and jealousy and wrangling and factions among you, are you not unspiritual and of the flesh, behaving yourselves after a human standard and like mere (unchanged) men?" (AMP)*

More scriptures attest to this:
But for those who are self-seeking and self-willed and disobedient to the Truth but responsive to wickedness, there will be indignation and wrath. (Romans 2:8, AMP)

But if you have bitter jealousy (envy) and contention (rivalry, selfish ambition) in your hearts, do not pride yourselves on it and thus be in defiance of and false to the Truth. (James 3:14)

God wants us to be content with what He has given to us. Inordinate ambitions breed all manners of evil. That is why the Bible says in 1 Timothy 6:6-8 *"But godliness with contentment is great gain. For we brought nothing into this world, and it is certain we can carry nothing out. And having food and raiment let us be therewith content."* God does not expect us to compare ourselves to one another and any one that does that is referred to as a fool.

2 Corinthians 10:12 says *"For we dare not make ourselves of the number, or compare ourselves with some that commend themselves: but they measuring themselves by themselves, and comparing themselves among themselves, are not wise."*

6. Wrath

Wrath can be simply defined as "Extreme anger."

Synonyms include fury and rage. Wrath may be described as inordinate and uncontrolled feelings of hatred and anger. Wrath, in its purest form, presents itself with self-destructiveness, violence, and hate that may provoke feuds that can go on for centuries.

Wrath may persist long after the person who did another a grievous wrong is dead. Feelings of anger can manifest in different ways, including impatience and violence.

God expects us to have self-control by trusting His Spirit. The Bible says in Ephesians 4:26-27 *"Be ye angry, and sin not: let not the sun go down upon your wrath."*

In Proverbs 29:11, the Bible says *"A fool uttereth all his mind: but a wise man keepeth it in till afterwards"* And verse 20 says, *"Seest thou a man that is hasty in his words? there is more hope of a fool than of him."*

Anger is sinful when it leads us to lose control so that, instead of being helpful to others, we become abusive, saying evil or hateful things intended to hurt them. Cain's anger against Abel as recorded in Genesis 4:4-8 is a typical example of foolish anger. When God rejected Cain's offering but accepted Abel's, Cain became angry and killed Abel.

Cain's anger was wrong, first because Abel had done nothing wrong. Anger at sin may be justified, but Cain was angry with someone who was righteous. Cain was the one who did wrong and was upset because God did not accept his conduct. Second, his anger was wrong because it led him to harm his brother.

It is not all anger that is sinful. In the Bible we can see many people that showed justifiable anger. For instance, God showed anger towards sin. Psalm 7:11 says, *"God judgeth the righteous, and God is angry with the wicked every day"* and Romans 1:18 says *"For the wrath of God is revealed from heaven against all ungodliness and unrighteousness of men, who hold the truth in unrighteousness."*

The Bible says Moses was meeker than anyone else on earth (Numbers 12:3), yet several times he acted rashly and spoke in great anger. In Exodus 11:4-8, Moses predicted that God would destroy all the firstborns in all Egypt. Moses was acting as God's spokesman, a responsibility that was quite sacred, yet he spoke "in great anger" on more than one occasion and it cost him dearly.

In Exodus 32:19-24, we read that while Moses was on Mt. Sinai receiving the law, the children of Israel worshiped a golden calf. When he returned from communing with God and saw this, *"Moses' anger became hot"* (Verse 19), so much so that other people could see that he was angry (Verse 22). He spoke and he punished the people in anger.

(Compare with Verses 25 - 29)

In Numbers 16:15, when Korah, Dathan and Abiram led a rebellion against Moses' leadership, *"Moses was very angry,"* spoke in anger (Verse 16) and even prayed to God in anger.

In Luke 19:45-46, the Bible says *"And He went into the temple, and began to cast out them that sold therein, and them that bought; Saying unto them, It is written, My house is the house of prayer: but ye have made it a den of thieves."*

7. Strife

Strife refers to "bitter disagreement over fundamental issues." It refers to vigorous or bitter conflict, discord, or antagonism. Strife is fighting and struggling against another person. It is sinful to be in strife with others. The book of Romans 12:18 says *"If it be possible, as much as lieth in you, live peaceably with all men."* In Matthew 22:36-40, Jesus taught his disciples about the golden rule which is: Loving God and Loving our neighbors as ourselves. Where there is love, strife will not thrive. See the following Scriptures.

Follow peace with all men, and holiness, without which no man shall see the Lord. (Hebrews 12:14)

Where no wood is, there the fire goeth out: so where there is no talebearer, the strife ceaseth. (Proverbs 26:20)

A froward man soweth strife: and a whisperer separateth chief friends. (Proverbs 16:28)

How do you deal with people that cause strife? The Bible says in Romans 16:17 gives us a clear directive: *"Now I beseech you, brethren, mark them which cause divisions and offences contrary to the doctrine which ye have learned; and avoid them."*

8. Seditions

Seditions refer to a conduct or speech that incites people to rebel against constituted authorities. It is rebellion against lawful authority. The word "sedition" is defined as actions or words intended to lead or encourage the overthrow of a person, group or state. Sedition in the Bible is classified as a criminal act that undermines the set authority placed by God, seeking to overthrow it. You may not see sedition publicly because it is subtle. It is often hidden within the people that walk around the leader or the person appointed by God. Everywhere you go, God has set an authority figure or a head. If you speak ill about the authority that God has placed, then you are rebelling against God. Man in his natural state detests authority. Rebellion began with Satan in the pre-adamic age, when he rebelled against God and deceived one-third of the angels into joining with him.

And there appeared another wonder in heaven; and behold a great red dragon, having seven heads and ten horns, and seven crowns on his heads. And his tail drew the third part of the stars of heaven, and did cast them to the earth: and the dragon stood before the woman who was ready to be delivered, to devour her child as soon as it was born. (Revelation 12:3-4)

As human beings, believers are not exempt from having differing opinions from people in authorities but how does the Bible expect us to deal with authorities? This Scripture tells us how.

I exhort therefore, that, first of all, supplications, prayers, intercessions, and giving of thanks, be made for all men; For kings, and for all that are in authority; that we may lead a quiet and peaceable life in all godliness and honesty. For this is good and acceptable in the sight of God our Savior. (1 Timothy 2:1-3)

9. Heresies

Heresy connotes a departure or deviation from the truth. Heresies are false doctrines that turn men from the truth. Satan deceived our first mother, Eve, to sin against God. He even used scripture to tempt Jesus Christ to sin against God. The devil uses the same strategy today by promoting another Jesus, another gospel, and another spirit to turn men from the truth.

In 2 Peter 2:1-2, the Bible says, *"But there were false prophets also among the people, even as there shall be false teachers among you, who privily shall bring in damnable heresies, even denying the Lord that bought them, and bring upon themselves swift destruction. And many shall follow their pernicious ways; by reason of whom the way of truth shall be evil spoken of."*

1 John 4:1-3 says, *"Beloved, believe not every spirit, but try the spirits whether they are of God: because many false prophets are gone out into the world. Hereby know ye the Spirit of God: Every spirit that confesseth that Jesus Christ is come in the flesh is of God: And every spirit that confesseth not that Jesus Christ is come in the flesh is not of God: and this is that spirit of antichrist, whereof ye have heard that it should come; and even now already is it in the world."*

2 Corinthians 11:3-4 says, *"But I fear, lest by any means, as the serpent beguiled Eve through his subtilty, so your minds should be corrupted from the simplicity that is in Christ. For if he that cometh preacheth another Jesus, whom we have not preached, or if ye receive another spirit, which ye have not received, or another gospel, which ye have not accepted, ye might well bear with him."*

How can one avoid heresies?

Only the right understanding of the Scriptures can protect you.

False teachers prey on the ignorant. When Satan tempted Jesus in the wilderness, Jesus responded the same way to each of the three heresies presented using the words: "*It is written.*" We should not allow personal views and opinions to replace what the Bible says. Jesus Christ was able to counter and withstand the temptations of Satan by saying "*It is written*" and then providing the correct application of Scripture.

10. Envying

Envy can be defined as a resentful emotion that "occurs when a person lacks another's (perceived) superior quality, achievement or possession and wishes." Envy is a desire to have a quality, possession, or other attribute belonging to someone else. It is a feeling of discontent and resentment aroused by and in conjunction with the desire for the possessions or qualities of another.

Envy is the Greek *"phthonos."* It is the feeling of displeasure produced by witnessing or hearing of the advantage or prosperity of others. It is further defined as having hatred or ill will. It is also a feeling of discontent because of another person's advantages, qualities or possessions. An envious person has a resentful dislike for someone else who has something that he desires.

Biblical examples of envying

1. Saul against David

The story of King Saul and David is a classic example of envy. David had become quite a warrior and the people had begun to recognize his accomplishments. In 1 Samuel 18:7, we read these words, *"...Saul has slain his thousands, And David his ten thousands."* Then the following verses read, *"...Saul was very angry, and the saying displeased him; and he said, 'They have ascribed to David ten thousands, and to me they have ascribed only thousands. Now what more can he have but the kingdom?' So Saul eyed David from that day forward."*

What a contrast of life. On one hand we find a wonderful, caring relationship between David and Jonathan, Saul's son, and on the other, a man who wanted nothing more than to see David die.

So what happens? Saul begins to burn within himself and it tears him up that David, and not he, is getting all the fame and popularity. Saul is the king! Saul wants the fame and honor of all the people but he realizes that David is getting them. This inward hate now possesses him and he begins to take every opportunity to remove David permanently so that he will once again be the one at the center of everyone's attention. This resulted in multiple attempts to kill David.

Envy takes root right in the heart of man. Once rooted, it will breed many more sins. Saul now alienates himself from God as he becomes selfish, self-willed and full of his own pride.

Envy is a sin that grows in the background of another's preeminence. The seed of envy is the fruit of another person's accomplishments. It is the dread that the accomplishments of others will tower above our own. This is exactly what Saul saw in his new rival David. It says in 1 Samuel 18:30, *"...And so it was, whenever they went out, that David behaved more wisely than all the servants of Saul, so that his name became highly esteemed."* David was a man that acted with prudence and with caution and as a result he prospered.

There are many features that mark the sin of envy. When you are full of envy, you become unreasonable. Saul could have still been a good king, a respected king, but he chose to "come apart" and became unreasonable in his actions.

Ingratitude is also a fruit of envy. David did a great thing for Israel by choosing to fight the giant Goliath when no one else would even dare to. Through the help of God, David conquered this giant of a man, and then later fought battles that he was sent on by Saul although Saul had ulterior motives. In addition, he soothed the distressing spirit of Saul with the music of his harp (1 Samuel 18:10). So where's the gratitude? When one is entrenched in envy, there is no gratitude.

Once envy entered the heart of Saul, he was on a downward course in his relationship with God and man. It destroyed him and prematurely ended a beautiful relationship between David and Jonathan.

2. Cain against Abel

Abel and Cain were brothers and they both had opportunities to give sacrificial offerings to God. Abel's offering was more acceptable to God than his brother's and Cain became envious wishing that God had accepted his own offering rather than his brother's. Envy led him to murder his own brother and he received an eternal curse from the Lord.

Envy is hurtful. When envy takes over, it is the person filled with this sin that ultimately pays the price. A person loses contentment, peace and joy in life when the mind is occupied with envy. The Christian needs to know that life does not consist in the material things but rather the spiritual. If we will put the following passages to use in our life, then we will not have to be concerned with envy making its home in our heart.

Therefore, whatever you want men to do to you, do also to them, for this is the Law and the Prophets. (Matthew 7:12)

Set your mind on things above, not on things on the earth. (Colossians 3:2)

And you shall love the LORD your God with all your heart, with all your soul, with all your mind, and with all your strength.' This is the first commandment. And the second, like it, is this: 'You shall love your neighbor as yourself.' There is no other commandment greater than these. (Mark 12:30-31)

The Danger of envying

Envy can be found everywhere today, even in the church. But wherever it appears, it is still envy and it is still sin. What is our reaction to those around us who have a high position in the ranks of society? How many times have we uttered, "I wish I had his job and pay?" Materialism breeds greed and envy. Envy dwells within the heart. It is a cancer that in a short time will eat away the fruit of the spirit found in Galatians 5:22-23.

Do not let your heart envy sinners, But be zealous for the fear of the LORD all the day. (Proverbs 23:17)

We must give caution to this terrible sin of envy. It led Jesus to be crucified because of its passion, a force that comes from within and directs our thinking and actions. It affects the entire man, for whatever is of the heart comes forth in life.

If you are envious of others, the one you will hurt the most by your actions will be you. This was true of the Jews who delivered up the Christ to be crucified and it was true of Saul who made it his life's mission to kill David. This is also true of anyone today who becomes envious of others. We must cultivate the kind of mind that the apostle Paul mentions in Romans 12:16-18: *'Be of the same mind toward one another. Do not set your mind on high things, but associate with the humble. Do not be wise in your own opinion. Repay no one evil for evil. Have regard for good things in the sight of all men. If it is possible, as much as depends on you, live peaceably with all men."*

11. Murders

When you forcefully and unlawfully take the life of another man; you have committed the sin of murder. In order for the act to be considered murder, the killing must be both premeditated and intentional. Exodus 20:13 says explicitly *"Thou shalt not kill"*. The Lord frowns seriously at the shedding of innocent blood. When Cain murdered his brother Abel, the Lord cursed him.

In Genesis 9:6 the Bible says, *"Whoso sheddeth man's blood, by man shall his blood be shed: for in the image of God made he man."*

Exodus 21:12 says, *"He that smiteth a man, so that he die, shall be surely put to death."*

In Matthew 26:52, the Bible says, *"Then said Jesus unto him, Put up again thy sword into his place: for all they that take the sword shall perish with the sword."*

People kill others because of vengeance. They want to take their pound of flesh but this is not scriptural.

The Bible says in Romans 12:19 says *"Dearly beloved, avenge not yourselves, but rather give place unto wrath: for it is written, Vengeance is mine; I will repay, saith the Lord."*

Abortion is murder because life begins at the embryonic stage; no man must kill what he did not make.

12. Drunkenness

Also known as alcoholic intoxication. The dictionary defines drunkenness as "a temporary state resulting from excessive consumption of alcohol." The scriptures clearly teach that drunkenness is sin (*Refer to Galatians 5:21*) and that drunkards will not inherit the kingdom of heaven (*Refer to 1 Corinthians 6:9-10*).

Drunkenness is indeed a sin but drinking a little wine is not. In fact the Bible tells us to drink a little wine for a healthy stomach and prevention of frequent ailments. 1 Timothy 5:23 says *"Drink no longer water, but use a little wine for thy stomach's sake and thine often infirmities."* However, we must be careful and must practice extra self-control not to drink too much wine, not to get drunk and not to be addicted to it.

In spiritual words, we must live spiritually and not be tempted by physical vices, such as drunkenness, which causes violence, loss of self-discipline, physical weakness, diseases and more.

13. Reveling

Reveling means:

1. To take great pleasure or delight

2. To engage in uproarious festivities; make merry.

A good example of reveling is if you go out to celebrate your graduation and you engage in excessive drinking, partying, raving and having a 'great' time. Also, if you watch your worst enemy get fired and you take great delight in the situation, this is an example of when you are reveling in your enemy's misfortune.

The dictionary defines reveling as a boisterous festivity or celebration or merrymaking. Let me be clear that it is not wrong for Christians to rejoice, to celebrate or to be happy, but it is wrong to drink, dance mindlessly, and engage in boisterous, unruly acts that are associated with drinking parties that often include drunkenness and sexual immorality. Faithful Christians must condemn riotous conduct and reveling of all kinds in thought, word and in deed.

And have no fellowship with the unfruitful works of darkness, but rather reprove them. For it is a shame even to speak of those things which are done of them in secret. (Eph. 5:11, 12)

They which do such things shall not inherit the kingdom of God. (Gal. 5:21)

God wants us to be moderate and sober in everything we do. Even in rejoicing, it must be done with moderation.

In Philippians 4:5, the Bible says *"Let your moderation be known unto all men. The Lord is at hand."*

Titus 2:12 says *"Teaching us that, denying ungodliness and worldly lusts, we should live soberly, righteously, and godly, in this present world."*

1 Peter 5:8 says *"Be sober, be vigilant; because your adversary the devil, as a roaring lion, walketh about, seeking whom he may devour."*

Chapter 4
The Ministry of the Holy Spirit

Having dealt with the fruit of the Spirit and the works of the flesh, it is important to have a thorough understanding of who the Holy Spirit is. It is sad that in our world today, many people, even Christians, still do not fully understand who the Holy Spirit is and the very important role He plays in our lives. This chapter is dedicated to helping you have a thorough understanding of the person and ministry of the Holy Spirit.

A. The Origin of the Holy Spirit

In the beginning God created the heaven and the earth. And the earth was without form, and void; and darkness was upon the face of the deep. And the Spirit of God moved upon the face of the waters. (Genesis 1:1-2)

From the above Scripture, it is obvious that all three persons of the Trinity were involved in Creation - the Father, the Son and the Holy Spirit.

God the Father delights in giving form to that which is formless and filling that which is empty. God the Father's assistant, in this great work, is the Holy Spirit.

The Holy Spirit is included in the Trinity, which is made up of 3 distinct persons: The Father, the Son, and the *Holy Spirit*.

The Holy Spirit is called by several names in the Bible:

The Spirit of God (*Genesis 1:2; Ephesians 4:30*).

The Spirit of the Lord (*Luke 4:18*).

The Spirit of His Son (*Galatians 4:6*).

The Spirit of Christ (*Romans 8:9*).

The Spirit of holiness (*Romans 1:4*).

The Spirit of grace and supplication (*Zechariah 12:10*).

The Spirit of wisdom and revelation (*Ephesians 1:17; Proverbs 8*).

The Spirit of understanding, counsel, power, knowledge and the fear of the Lord (*Isaiah 11:2*).

The Spirit of truth (*John 14:17; 15:26*).

The Spirit of love, power and self-discipline (*2 Timothy 1:7*).

The Spirit of sonship (*Romans 8:15*).

The Counselor (*John 14:16*).

The Holy Spirit (*Acts 1:5, 8; 2:1-4*).

B. Characteristics of the Holy Spirit

Firstly, the Holy Spirit has the Characteristic of Personality:

1. The Holy Spirit has a Mind:

The Holy Spirit is not a mere force and is not an "it" as some refer to Him. He has a mind.

And he who searches our hearts knows the mind of the Spirit, because the Spirit intercedes for the saints in accordance with God's will. (Romans 8:27)

2. The Holy Spirit has a Will:

The Holy Spirit also has a will, can process information and make decisions. He is an active Spirit that is relational.

But one and the same Spirit works all these things, distributing to each one individually just as He wills. (1 Corinthians 12:11)

3. The Holy Spirit has Emotions:

The Bible makes it very clear that it is possible to grieve the Holy Spirit. This also means that the Holy Spirit has feelings and can be happy or grieved based on our actions or inactions. This does not mean however that the Holy Spirit acts on impulse or based on emotions.

And do not grieve the Holy Spirit of God, with whom you were sealed for the day of redemption. (Ephesians 4:30)

Yet they rebelled and grieved his Holy Spirit. So he turned and became their enemy and he himself fought against them. (Isaiah 63:10)

4. The Holy Spirit gives joy:

Jesus referred to the Holy Spirit as the Comforter. He is a joyful Spirit that gives us joy in the midst of storms and trouble. He calms the broken hearted, strengthens the hearts and minds of those who call on the Lord.

At that time Jesus, full of joy through the Holy Spirit, said, "I praise you, Father, Lord of heaven and earth, because you have hidden these things from the wise and learned, and revealed them to little children. Yes, Father, for this was your good pleasure. (Luke 10: 21)

You became imitators of us and of the Lord; in spite of severe suffering, you welcomed the message with the joy given by the Holy Spirit. (1 Thessalonians 1:6)

5. The Holy Spirit Teaches:

The Holy Spirit is the greatest teacher in the entire universe. He knows everything and searches even the deep things of God.

But the Counselor, the Holy Spirit, whom the Father will send in my name, will teach you all things and will remind you of everything I have said to you. (John 14:26, NIV)

6. The Holy Spirit Testifies of Christ:

The Holy Spirit is a guide that always points us to Jesus.

When the Counselor comes, whom I will send to you from the Father, the Spirit of truth who goes out from the Father, he will testify about me. (John 15:26, NIV)

7. The Holy Spirit Convicts:

The Bible clearly states that the Holy Spirit convicts of sin.

When he comes, he will convict the world of guilt (Or will expose the guilt of the world) in regard to sin and righteousness and judgment. (John 16:8, NIV)

8. The Holy Spirit Leads:

Being led by the Spirit means yielding our will to God's perfect plan and it is a daily act of surrendering to the leadership of the Holy Spirit. The Holy Spirit speaks to us and leads us.

Because those who are led by the Spirit of God are sons of God. (Romans 8:14)

9. The Holy Spirit Reveals Truth:

A phenomenal attribute of the Holy Spirit is that He reveals the truth. This is why it is so critical to understand the workings of the Holy Spirit so you can live an overcoming life. God reveals the future to us through the Holy Spirit.

There are countless stories of miracles and avoidance of death or accidents simply because of yielding to the directives of the Holy Spirit. The opposite of this is soothsaying and familiar spirits as discussed in the preceding chapter.

But when he, the Spirit of truth, comes, he will guide you into all truth. He will not speak on his own; he will speak only what he hears, and he will tell you what is yet to come. (John 16:13)

10. The Holy Spirit Strengthens and Encourages:

Countless times in the New Testament church, we see the Holy Spirit at work strengthening and comforting the Christians who were facing grave persecution. There is no encourager like the Holy Spirit.

Then the church throughout Judea, Galilee and Samaria enjoyed a time of peace. It was strengthened; and encouraged by the Holy Spirit, it grew in numbers, living in the fear of the Lord. (Acts 9:31)

11. The Holy Spirit Comforts:

The Holy Spirit comforts us and gives us peace in the most difficult situations. It is sad that even believers struggle through depression, anxiety and sadness when the Spirit of God can liberate and give us calm in the midst of life's many storms.

And I will pray the Father, and he shall give you another Comforter, that he may abide with you forever. (John 14:16)

12. The Holy Spirit Helps Us in our Weakness:

In the same way, the Spirit helps us in our weakness. We do not know what we ought to pray for, but the Spirit himself intercedes for us with groans that words cannot express. (Romans 8:26)

13. The Holy Spirit Intercedes:

In the same way, the Spirit helps us in our weakness. We do not know what we ought to pray for, but the Spirit himself intercedes for us with groans that words cannot express. (Romans 8:26)

14. The Holy Spirit Searches the Deep Things of God:

The Spirit searches all things, even the deep things of God. For who among men knows the thoughts of a man except the man's spirit within him? In the same way no one knows the thoughts of God except the Spirit of God. (1 Corinthians 2:11)

15. The Holy Spirit Sanctifies:

To be a minister of Christ Jesus to the Gentiles with the priestly duty of proclaiming the gospel of God, so that the Gentiles might become an offering acceptable to God, sanctified by the Holy Spirit. (Romans 15:16)

16. The Holy Spirit Bears Witness or Testifies:

The Spirit itself beareth witness with our spirit, that we are the children of God. (Romans 8:16)

17. The Holy Spirit Forbids:

Paul and his companions traveled throughout the region of Phrygia and Galatia, having been kept by the Holy Spirit from preaching the word in the province of Asia. When they came to the border of Mysia, they tried to enter Bithynia, but the Spirit of Jesus would not allow them to. (Acts 16:6-7)

18. The Holy Spirit can be lied to:

Then Peter said, "Ananias, how is it that Satan has so filled your heart that you have lied to the Holy Spirit and have kept for yourself some of the money you received for the land? (Acts 5:3)

19. The Holy Spirit can be resisted:

You stiff-necked people, with uncircumcised hearts and ears! You are just like your fathers: You always resist the Holy Spirit! (Acts 7:51)

20. The Holy Spirit can be blasphemed:

And so I tell you, every sin and blasphemy will be forgiven men, but the blasphemy against the Spirit *will not be forgiven. Anyone who speaks a word against the Son of Man will be forgiven, but anyone who speaks against the Holy Spirit will not be forgiven, either in this age or in the age to come.* (Matthew 12:31-32)

21. The Holy Spirit can be quenched:

Quench not the Spirit. (1 Thessalonians 5:19)

C. The Holy Spirit and Jesus' Ministry

The Holy Spirit was fully involved in the entire life of Jesus Christ from conception to birth, to growing up, from ministry to death, resurrection and ascension. In the first chapter of the book of Luke, after Angel Gabriel brought the good news about the birth of Jesus to Mary and she was confused since she was a virgin, the Bible says in verses 34-35, *"Then said Mary unto the angel, How shall this be, seeing I know not a man? And the angel answered and said unto her, The Holy Ghost shall come upon thee, and the power of the Highest shall overshadow thee: therefore also that holy thing which shall be born of thee shall be called the Son of God."*

The Holy Ghost and God's power upon Mary preceded His conception. Jesus grew up as a child in partnership with the Holy Spirit. In Luke 2:52, the Bible says, *"And Jesus increased in wisdom and stature, and in favor with God and man."* John the Baptist also prophesied that Jesus was going to be the link between man and the Holy Ghost.

And as the people were in expectation, and all men mused in their hearts of John, whether he were the Christ, or not; John answered, saying unto them all, I indeed baptize you with water; but one mightier than I cometh, the latchet of whose shoes I am not worthy to unloose: he shall baptize you with the Holy Ghost and with fire. (Luke 3:15-16)

John baptized many of the people but as soon as Jesus was baptized, the Bible recalls that the Holy Ghost came upon him as a dove.

Now when all the people were baptized, it came to pass, that Jesus also being baptized, and praying, the heaven was opened. And the Holy Ghost descended in a bodily shape like a dove upon him, and a voice came from heaven, which said, Thou art my beloved Son; in thee I am well pleased. (Luke 3:22)

Jesus thereafter commenced his ministry in Luke 4:1 partnering with the same Holy Spirit.

And Jesus being full of the Holy Ghost returned from Jordan, and was led by the Spirit into the wilderness. (Luke 4:1)

And in verse 14, the Bible says, "*And Jesus returned in the power of the Spirit into Galilee: and there went out a fame of him through all the region roundabout.*"

In verses 18 and 19, he quoted the prophecy in the book of Isaiah:

The Spirit of the Lord is upon me, because he hath anointed me to preach the gospel to the poor; he hath sent me to heal the brokenhearted, to preach deliverance to the captives, and recovering of sight to the blind, to set at liberty them that are bruised, To preach the acceptable year of the Lord. (Isaiah 61:1)

He did not just partner with the Holy Ghost to do the work of the ministry; He also taught His disciples how to work with the Holy Spirit. In Luke 12:10-12, the Bible says, "*And whosoever shall speak a word against the Son of man, it shall be forgiven him: but unto him that blasphemeth against the Holy Ghost it shall not be forgiven. And when they bring you unto the synagogues, and unto magistrates, and powers, take ye no thought how or what thing ye shall answer, or what ye shall say: For the Holy Ghost shall teach you in the same hour what ye ought to say.*"

In John 14:16-18, Jesus informed his disciples of His imminent departure and He promised them of the coming of the Comforter who is also the Holy Ghost.

And I will pray the Father, and he shall give you another Comforter, that he may abide with you forever; Even the Spirit of truth; whom the world cannot receive, because it seeth him not, neither knoweth him: but ye know him; for he dwelleth with you, and shall be in you. I will not leave you comfortless: I will come to you. (John 14:16-18)

He continued in verse 26 that, "*…the Comforter, which is the Holy Ghost, whom the Father will send in my name, he shall teach you all things, and bring all things to your remembrance, whatsoever I have said unto you.*"

Jesus also taught his disciples about the roles of the Holy Spirit:

I have yet many things to say unto you, but ye cannot bear them now. Howbeit when he, the Spirit of truth, is come, he will guide you into all truth: for he shall not speak of himself; but whatsoever he shall hear, that shall he speak: and he will shew you things to come. He shall glorify me: for he shall receive of mine, and shall shew it unto you. All things that the Father hath are mine: therefore said I, that he shall take of mine, and shall shew it unto you. A little while, and ye shall not see me: and again, a little while, and ye shall see me, because I go to the Father. (John 16:12-16)

D. The Holy Spirit and Power

And when he had said this, he breathed on them, and saith unto them, Receive ye the Holy Ghost. (John 20:22)

After Jesus ascended, the Bible says He gave them the Holy Ghost, which is a process every believer must go through for salvation to be complete. This event is different from the one in Acts 1 where they were baptized in the Holy Ghost.

But ye shall receive power, after that the Holy Ghost is come upon you: and ye shall be witnesses unto me both in Jerusalem, and in all Judæa, and in Samaria, and unto the uttermost part of the earth. (Acts 1:8)

And, being assembled together with them, commanded them that they should not depart from Jerusalem, but wait for the promise of the Father, which, saith he, ye have heard of me. For John truly baptized with water; but ye shall be baptized with the Holy Ghost not many days hence. (Acts 1:4-5)

What does it mean to be "baptized in the Holy Ghost?"

To be baptized means to be "completely immersed in a thing." It is a process of initiation or adoption through an exercise of total dipping. Up until that moment, what was known *as* baptism was a ritual done by immersing into water which was popularly done by John the Baptist, but Jesus was letting his disciples know that until a believer is baptized in the Holy Ghost, empowerment is not complete. While baptism by immersion symbolizes your adoption as a child of God, baptism in the Holy Ghost empowers you to manifest sonship. That is why the Bible says in Romans 8:14-15, "*For as many as are led by the Spirit of God, they are the sons of God. For ye have not received the spirit of bondage again to fear; but ye have received the Spirit of adoption, whereby we cry, Abba, Father.*"

In verse 7, the disciples were concerned about issues of religion and different fables of their fathers, the restoration of the kingdom to Israel but Jesus redirected them to focus on a more important issue, which is "Divine Empowerment."

When you receive the Holy Ghost and His divine power, you will become witnesses of Jesus and the kingdom of His father. A witness is someone that testifies about an event or a person to others. A witness can also be defined as "*one who can give a firsthand account of something seen, heard, or experienced.*"

Talking about power, two scriptures already prophesied the imminent release of divine power on as many as believe in Jesus. In Joel 2:28-32, the Bible says *"And it shall come to pass afterward, that I will pour out my spirit upon all flesh; and your sons and your daughters shall prophesy, your old men shall dream dreams, your young men shall see visions: And also upon the servants and upon the handmaids in those days will I pour out my spirit. And I will shew wonders in the heavens and in the earth, blood, and fire, and pillars of smoke. The sun shall be turned into darkness, and the moon into blood, before the great and the terrible day of the Lord come. And it shall come to pass, that whosoever shall call on the name of the Lord shall be delivered: for in mount Zion and in Jerusalem shall be deliverance, as the Lord hath said, and in the remnant whom the Lord shall call."*

Secondly, Jesus already told the disciples in Mark 16:15-18 that they would be able to do similar miracles and supernatural acts like He did.

And he said unto them, Go ye into all the world, and preach the gospel to every creature. He that believeth and is baptized shall be saved; but he that believeth not shall be damned. And these signs shall follow them that believe; In my name shall they cast out devils; they shall speak with new tongues; They shall take up serpents; and if they drink any deadly thing, it shall not hurt them; they shall lay hands on the sick, and they shall recover. (Mark 16:15-18)

In essence, Jesus was telling them that the baptism of the Holy Ghost would empower them and give them the ability to:

1. Preach the gospel with boldness and authority.

2. Cast out devils from those that are oppressed.

3. Speak in new tongues.

4. Dare the devil and be free from the consequences of doing so.

5. Lay hands on the sick and the sick to recover.

I submit to you that until a child of God is able to demonstrate the power of God in this manner, he is not a true witness of Christ and His kingdom.

E. The Mystery of Tongues

Of all the five manifestations of divine power mentioned above, the one that is most controversial is speaking in tongues. To fully understand the concept of tongues, we have to study its origin in Acts Chapter 2 on the day now called *"The day of Pentecost."*

Pentecost is significant in both the Old and New Testaments. "Pentecost" is actually the Greek name for a festival known in the Old Testament as the Feast of Weeks. This name comes from an expression in Leviticus 23:16, which instructs people to count seven weeks or "fifty days" from the end of Passover to the beginning of the next holiday. It was originally a harvest festival (Exodus 23:16), but, in time, turned into a day to commemorate the giving of the law on Mt. Sinai. This day became especially significant for Christians because, seven weeks after the resurrection of Jesus, during the Jewish celebration of Pentecost, the Holy Spirit was poured out upon his first followers, thus empowering them for their mission and gathering them together as a church.

In Acts 2:1-14 the Bible says:

"And when the day of Pentecost was fully come, they were all with one accord in one place. And suddenly there came a sound from heaven as of a rushing mighty wind, and it filled all the house where they were sitting. And there appeared unto

them cloven tongues like as of fire, and it sat upon each of them. And they were all filled with the Holy Ghost, and began to speak with other tongues, as the Spirit gave them utterance. And there were dwelling at Jerusalem Jews, devout men, out of every nation under heaven. Now when this was noised abroad, the multitude came together, and were confounded, because that every man heard them speak in his own language. And they were all amazed and marvelled, saying one to another, Behold, are not all these which speak Galilæans? And how hear we every man in our own tongue, wherein we were born? Parthians, and Medes, and Elamites, and the dwellers in Mesopotamia, and in Judæa, and Cappadocia, in Pontus, and Asia, Phrygia, and Pamphylia, in Egypt, and in the parts of Libya about Cyrene, and strangers of Rome, Jews and proselytes, Cretes and Arabians, we do hear them speak in our tongues the wonderful works of God. And they were all amazed, and were in doubt, saying one to another, What meaneth this? Others mockingsaid, These men are full of new wine."

Certain truths can be established from the above scriptures concerning tongues:

1. It was a fulfillment of prophecy.

2. It is a physical and outward manifestation of the presence of an inward power in a believer.

3. No man can learn to speak in tongues. It is given supernaturally by the Holy Ghost to them that believe.

4. It is different from the gift of diverse tongues.

   To another the working of miracles; to another prophecy; to another discerning of spirits; to another divers kinds of tongues; to another the interpretation of tongues… (1 Corinthians 12:10)

5. Except if one is given the gift of interpretation of tongues,

you will not understand what is being spoken in tongues.

F. Receiving the baptism of the Holy Ghost

God wants to give the gift of the Holy Spirit to as many of his children that ask. In Luke 11:9-13, the Bible says *"And I say unto you, Ask, and it shall be given you; seek, and ye shall find; knock, and it shall be opened unto you. For every one that asketh receiveth; and he that seeketh findeth; and to him that knocketh it shall be opened. If a son shall ask bread of any of you that is a father, will he give him a stone? or if he ask a fish, will he for a fish give him a serpent? Or if he shall ask an egg, will he offer him a scorpion? If ye then, being evil, know how to give good gifts unto your children: how much more shall your heavenly Father give the Holy Spirit to them that ask him?"*

There must therefore first be an asking before there can be a giving.

And it came to pass, that, while Apollos was at Corinth, Paul having passed through the upper coasts came to Ephesus: and finding certain disciples, He said unto them, Have ye received the Holy Ghost since ye believed? And they said unto him, We have not so much as heard whether there be any Holy Ghost. And he said unto them, Unto what then were ye baptized? And they said, Unto John's baptism. Then said Paul, John verily baptized with the baptism of repentance, saying unto the people, that they should believe on him which should come after him, that is, on Christ Jesus. When they heard this, they were baptized in the name of the Lord Jesus. And when Paul had laid his hands upon them, the Holy Ghost came on them; and they spake with tongues, and prophesied. (Acts 19:1-6)

One can see a process of ministration carried out by Paul before the disciples received the baptism of the Holy Ghost.

1. He taught them the doctrine of baptism, clearly distinguishing between water baptism and Holy Ghost baptism. The Bible says *"the entrance of your word, it bringeth light, and it bringeth*

understanding to the simple." (Psalm 119:130)

2.   He laid his hands upon them.

3.   The recipients were expectant and this triggered faith in them. No man receives anything from God without faith.

While it is a sign of the baptism of the Holy Ghost, tongues are not the only way of showing that one has the Holy Ghost though it is a good gift to covet for several reasons:

1.   It improves our prayer life.

> Romans 8:26-27 says *"Likewise the Spirit also helpeth our infirmities: for we know not what we should pray for as we ought: but the Spirit itself maketh intercession for us with groanings which cannot be uttered. he that searcheth the hearts knoweth what is the mind of the Spirit, because he maketh intercession for the saints according to the will of God."*

> Partnering with the Holy Ghost in prayer is a crucial function of the Holy Ghost. We are too weak physically and spiritually to pray on our own except the spirit helps us.

2.   It helps to build our faith.

> Jude 20 says *"But ye, beloved, building up yourselves on your most holy faith, praying in the Holy Ghost."* When you pray regularly in the spirit, the grace to trust God increases and your faith increases. To pray in a language your mind does not understand, that so many make fun of, that the devil even tells you again and again, "You are just making that up" or "You are just wasting your time," takes faith.

Sometimes you do not even feel like praying, yet you speak in tongues and yes, this takes faith. If you want a muscle to grow, you have to use it and stretch it out. Likewise, if you want your faith to grow, you have to use it and stretch it. Every time you pray in tongues, you do just that.

3. Speaking in tongues edifies the believer.

1 Corinthians 14:4 says, *"He who speaks in a tongue edifies himself"*. "Praying in the Spirit" helps your spirit man grow stronger. When you speak in tongues regularly, you are building a spiritual legacy with your life. "Build yourself up" daily by praying in tongues.

4. Mysterious problems of life are solved when you speak in tongues regularly.

For he who speaks in a tongue does not speak to men but to God, for no one understands him; however, in the spirit he speaks mysteries. (1 Cor. 14:2)

Life is full of mysteries and many unanswered questions. How am I going to get rid of this pain in my body? What can I do to help my kid get off drugs? How can I overcome this sin? What should I do to pay this bill? How can I save this marriage? The Holy Spirit knows the answer to every mystery and that is why He is called the *"Spirit of truth."* (Refer to John 15:13)

1 Corinthians 2:9-11 says *"But as it is written, Eye hath not seen, nor ear heard, neither have entered into the heart of man, the things which God hath prepared for them that love him. But God hath revealed them unto us by his Spirit: for the Spirit searcheth all things, yea, the deep*

things of God. For what man knoweth the things of a man, save the spirit of man which is in him? even so the things of God knoweth no man, but the Spirit of God."

The answer to the mystery has not "entered your heart" just yet. But, God "has prepared" something special for you. It is way too "deep" for your mind to comprehend but you have a "Helper" in the Holy Spirit. And, He "searches all things (He knows where to shine the searchlight of His knowledge on a darkened subject)."

Thus, every time you pray in the Spirit, you are allowing the Holy Spirit to help you "search" out (research) the answer to your mysteries. You are entering the research laboratory of life and you will definitely come out with great results.

5. Tongues help us to pray more accurately.

In Romans 8:26-28, the Bible says *"Likewise the Spirit also helpeth our infirmities: for we know not what we should pray for as we ought: but the Spirit itself maketh intercession for us with groanings which cannot be uttered. And he that searcheth the hearts knoweth what is the mind of the Spirit, because he maketh intercession for the saints according to the will of God. And we know that all things work together for good to them that love God, to them who are the called according to his purpose."*

Every time you pray in tongues, you allow the Holy Spirit to take over your prayer life and intercede "for" you. You may be burdened about your finances and praying earnestly about that but God may see that that is the least of your problems. So, He has given you a precious gift through the Holy Spirit enabling you to pray for the really pressing need. The real need "cannot be uttered" by you in your native speech, simply because you are unaware of the seriousness of that area of need so the Holy Spirit carries the burden for you with "groaning."

You cannot groan about it, because you are ignorant of it. But the Spirit, full of love and compassion, uses your tongue as a tool to carry the need to the Father and He groans for you. What does groaning mean? "Making a deep inarticulate sound in response to pain or despair" What changes need to come to your life, your church's life, your children's life, your country's life? You may be unaware of the urgency for changes to come, but the Spirit isn't. He is waiting for you to in faith allow Him the privilege to "groan" through you in intercessory prayer to change the world around you.

6. Speaking in tongues is a weapon of spiritual warfare.

    2 Corinthians 10:3-6 says *"For though we walk in the flesh, we do not war after the flesh:(For the weapons of our warfare are not carnal, but mighty through God to the pulling down of strong holds;)Casting down imaginations, and every high thing that exalteth itself against the knowledge of God, and bringing into captivity every thought to the obedience of Christ; And having in a readiness to revenge all disobedience, when your obedience is fulfilled."*

    As believers, we would be deceiving ourselves if we do not accept the fact that life itself is spiritual warfare. There is always a continuous contention between light and darkness and we are daily engaged in this warfare.

    Paul teaching about spiritual warfare in Ephesians 6:10-18 said *"Finally, my brethren, be strong in the Lord, and in the power of his might. Put on the whole armor of God that ye may be able to stand against the wiles of the devil. For we wrestle not against flesh and blood, but against principalities, against powers, against the rulers of the darkness of this world, against spiritual wickedness in high places. Wherefore take unto you the whole armor of God, that ye may be able to withstand in the evil day, and having done all, to stand. Stand therefore, having your loins girt about with truth, and having on the breastplate of righteousness; And your feet shod with the preparation of the gospel of peace; Above all, taking the shield of faith, wherewith ye shall be able to quench all the fiery darts of the wicked. And take the helmet of salvation, and the sword of the Spirit, which is the word of God: Praying always with all prayer and supplication in the Spirit, and watching thereunto with all perseverance and supplication for all saints."*

Prayer is listed as one of the tools we use to defeat Satan. Paul qualified   prayer by saying "with all prayer and supplication in the Spirit." Prayer must not just be led by the spirit but also conducted in the language of the spirit. It is easy to see how praying in tongues would be one of the most powerful weapons of warfare against the devil. When you pray in the Holy Spirit, you allow the Spirit (who sees exactly what the devil is up to in the invisible) help you pray against his attacks. When you know where and when the devil is in action, take authority over him in Jesus name claiming the promises and the power of the blood. But, when the devil is lurking in dark corners, be assured that every time you pray in tongues, you're unmasking him through the power of the Holy Spirit! Prepare your heart to be ready at any time to stop whatever you are doing to partner with the Holy Spirit when He determines the need has arisen.

G. Abuse of tongues

Like every good thing, the tendency for abuse is highly inevitable. Having looked at the benefits of tongues, one can expect that men will inadvertently abuse it. We would look at some fundamental issues about tongues and abuse as explained by Apostle Paul in his epistle to the church in Corinth in 1 Corinthians 14.

1. Prophecy versus Tongues

To understand this topic, we need to do an in-depth study of 1 Corinthians 14. For easy referencing, here are verses 2 to 11 and verses 21 to 33.

2 For he that speaketh in an unknown tongue speaketh not unto men, but unto God: for no man understandeth him; howbeit in the spirit he speaketh mysteries.
3 But he that prophesieth speaketh unto men to edification, and exhortation, and comfort.
4 He that speaketh in an unknown tongue edifieth himself; but he that prophesieth edifieth the church.
5 I would that ye all spake with tongues, but rather that ye prophesied: for greater is he that prophesieth than he that speaketh with tongues, except he interpret, that the church may receive edifying.
6 Now, brethren, if I come unto you speaking with tongues, what shall I profit you, except I shall speak to you either by revelation, or by knowledge, or by prophesying, or by doctrine?
7 And even things without life giving sound, whether pipe or harp, except they give a distinction in the sounds, how shall it be known what is piped or harped?
8 For if the trumpet give an uncertain sound, who shall prepare himself to the battle?
9 So likewise ye, except ye utter by the tongue words easy to be understood, how shall it be known what is spoken? for ye shall speak into the air.

10 There are, it may be, so many kinds of voices in the world, and none of them is without signification.

11 Therefore if I know not the meaning of the voice, I shall be unto him that speaketh a barbarian, and he that speaketh shall be a barbarian unto me.

21 In the law it is written, With men of other tongues and other lips will I speak unto this people; and yet for all that will they not hear me, saith the Lord.

22 Wherefore tongues are for a sign, not to them that believe, but to them that believe not: but prophesying serveth not for them that believe not, but for them which believe.

23 If therefore the whole church be come together into one place, and all speak with tongues, and there come in those that are unlearned, or unbelievers, will they not say that ye are mad?

24 But if all prophesy, and there come in one that believeth not, or one unlearned, he is convinced of all, he is judged of all:

25 And thus are the secrets of his heart made manifest; and so falling down on his face he will worship God, and report that God is in you of a truth.

26 How is it then, brethren? when ye come together, every one of you hath a psalm, hath a doctrine, hath a tongue, hath a revelation, hath an interpretation. Let all things be done unto edifying.

27 If any man speak in an unknown tongue, let it be by two, or at the most by three, and that by course; and let one interpret.

28 But if there be no interpreter, let him keep silence in the church; and let him speak to himself, and to God.

29 Let the prophets speak two or three, and let the other judge.

30 If any thing be revealed to another that sitteth by, let the first hold his peace.

31 For ye may all prophesy one by one, that all may learn, and all may be comforted.

32 And the spirits of the prophets are subject to the prophets.

33 For God is not the author of confusion, but of peace, as in all churches of the saints

(1 Corinthians 14)

Some basic truths can be established from the above 21 verses:

a. Tongues are not spoken to men by men but to God by men. God understands your tongues but men don't. (*Verse 2*)

b. Prophecies are given by men to men in understandable language to edify, exhort and comfort one another. Tongues, on the other hand, are spoken by man to God to edify (improve, encourage and lift up) oneself. (*Verses 3-4*)

c. He that prophesies is greater than he that speaks in tongues because prophecies edify others while tongues edify the speaker. (*Verses 5*)

d. There is no point speaking to people in tongues while there is no one to interpret for them to be edified. (*Verses 6-11*)

e. Tongues are spoken directly to God. If no one can interpret, do not speak in tongues to men. (*Verse 28*)

f. Though prophecy is to the public, it should still be done in order. (*Verse 29-33*)

2. Prayers Vs. Tongues

14 For if I pray in an unknown tongue, my spirit prayeth, but my understanding is unfruitful.

15 What is it then? I will pray with the spirit, and I will pray with the understanding also: I will sing with the spirit, and I will sing with the understanding also.

16 Else when thou shalt bless with the spirit, how shall he that occupieth the room of the unlearned say Amen at thy giving of thanks, seeing he understandeth not what thou sayest?

17 For thou verily givest thanks well, but the other is not edified.

(I Corinthians 14: 14-17)

    a. Praying in tongues is engaging the spirit to pray on my behalf. *(Verse 14)*

    b. The fact that you pray and sing in the spirit does not mean you are less spiritual when you pray and sing in understanding. By so doing, you bless both yourself and others. *(Verses 15-17)*

Chapter 5
Practical Acts of the Holy Spirit

We shall be looking at the various demonstration of the Holy Spirit to fully appreciate His relevance in the life of a believer.

1. His work in the conception of Christ

And in the sixth month the angel Gabriel was sent from God unto a city of Galilee, named Nazareth, To a virgin espoused to a man whose name was Joseph, of the house of David; and the virgin's name was Mary. And the angel came in unto her, and said, Hail, thou that art highly favoured, the Lord is with thee: blessed art thou among women. And when she saw him, she was troubled at his saying, and cast in her mind what manner of salutation this should be.

And the angel said unto her, Fear not, Mary: for thou hast found favour with God. And, behold, thou shalt conceive in thy womb, and bring forth a son, and shalt call his name JESUS.

He shall be great, and shall be called the Son of the Highest: and the Lord God shall give unto him the throne of his father David: And he shall reign over the house of Jacob for ever; and of his kingdom there shall be no end.

Then said Mary unto the angel, How shall this be, seeing I know not a man? And the angel answered and said unto her, The Holy Ghost shall come upon thee, and the power of the Highest shall overshadow thee: therefore also that holy thing which shall be born of thee shall be called the Son of God.

And, behold, thy cousin Elisabeth, she hath also conceived a son in her old age: and this is the sixth month with her, who was called barren. For with God nothing shall be impossible. (Luke1:26-37)

The Holy Ghost is the executor of the divine trust. When something unnatural was announced to Mary; she exclaimed "how shall this be?" Then the angel answered *"the Holy Ghost shall come upon thee."* (Acts 1:8)

When the Holy Ghost comes upon a natural man, supernatural results are produced. There are many amazing things that God wants to do on earth through simple vessels like Mary. Such acts will only be carried out through the Holy Ghost. It is naturally impracticable for a woman to conceive without the participation of a man. It is also naturally impossible for any man to walk on water like Jesus did or multiply five loaves of bread and two fishes to feed the hungry multitude. God, even now, is doing many of such mysterious things through the Holy Ghost.

2. The Day of Pentecost

And when the day of Pentecost was fully come, they were all with one accord in one place. And suddenly there came a sound from heaven as of a rushing mighty wind, and it filled all the house where they were sitting.

And there appeared unto them cloven tongues like as of fire, and it sat upon each of them. And they were all filled with the Holy Ghost, and began to speak with other tongues, as the Spirit gave them utterance.

And there were dwelling at Jerusalem Jews, devout men, out of every nation under heaven. Now when this was noised abroad, the multitude came together, and were confounded, because that every man heard them speak in his own language.

And they were all amazed and marvelled, saying one to another, Behold, are not all these which speak Galilæans? And how hear we every man in our own tongue, wherein we were born? (Acts 2:1-8)

Prior to this day and before Jesus ascended to heaven, He had already instructed his disciples to remain in Jerusalem until they were endued or clothed with power. Mysterious as it was, the disciples knew to obey than to ask too many questions.

One hundred and twenty of them waited in the upper room in one accord. Suddenly, there came a loud noise like a mighty rushing wind and cloven tongues as of fire upon them and they spoke in unknown tongues as the Spirit gave them utterance.

How could they just start speaking a language that had not been learnt? Even the people that heard those tongues testified that they were speaking in their native tongues.

If we yield our lives to the Holy Ghost, He will do mysterious things that will amaze every onlooker. God wants to use what He has given to us to do the supernatural; not just our tongues but also our intellect, our gifts and our time. Everything He has given to us should be released to Him to do more than what we are naturally capable of doing.

3. The man by the gate called beautiful delivered

Now Peter and John went up together into the temple at the hour of prayer, being the ninth hour. And a certain man lame from his mother's womb was carried, whom they laid daily at the gate of the temple which is called Beautiful, to ask alms of them that entered into the temple; Who seeing Peter and John about to go into the temple asked an alms. And Peter, fastening his eyes upon him with John, said, Look on us. And he gave heed unto them, expecting to receive something of them.

Then Peter said, Silver and gold have I none; but such as I have give I thee: In the name of Jesus Christ of Nazareth rise up and walk. And he took him by the right hand, and lifted him up: and immediately his feet and ankle bones received strength. And he leaping up stood, and walked, and entered with them into the temple, walking, and leaping, and praising God. And all the people saw him walking and praising God: And they knew that it was he which sat for alms at the Beautiful gate of the temple: and they were filled with wonder and amazement at that which had happened unto him. And as the lame man which was healed held Peter and John, all the people ran together unto them in the porch that is called Solomon's, greatly wondering. (Acts 3:1-12)

Peter and John have been coming to this temple and the lame man had always been sitting by the gate of the temple. It was the Holy Ghost that prompted them to pay attention to the man. Through the guidance of the Holy Ghost, things you have neglected before now will suddenly attract your attention.

The Holy Ghost is not concerned with the history of any disability. The man had been lame from his mother's womb and was completely dependent on others to get to the temple. The Apostles redirected his focus from what he was used to which was begging for alms. They had something else that the man never knew was his real need and that was "the name of Jesus." He wanted something physical but they had something spiritual for him. He wanted something temporal but they had something permanent for him. The Holy Ghost emboldened the Apostles to minister healing to him and the Holy Ghost made him to respond to the ministration and walk.

4. Ministering the word with power

And as they spake unto the people, the priests, and the captain of the temple, and the Sadducees, came upon them, being grieved that they taught the people, and preached through Jesus the resurrection from the dead.

And they laid hands on them, and put them in hold unto the next day: for it was now eventide. Howbeit many of them which heard the word believed; and the number of the men was about five thousand. And it came to pass on the morrow, that their rulers, and elders, and scribes, and Annas the high priest, and Caiaphas, and John, and Alexander, and as many as were of the kindred of the high priest, were gathered together at Jerusalem. And when they had set them in the midst, they asked, By what power, or by what name, have ye done this?

Then Peter, filled with the Holy Ghost, said unto them, Ye rulers of the people, and elders of Israel, if we this day be examined of the good deed done to the impotent man, by what means he is made whole; be it known unto you all, and to all the people of Israel, that by the name of Jesus Christ of Nazareth, whom ye crucified, whom God raised from the dead, even by him doth this man stand here before you whole.

This is the stone which was set at nought of you builders, which is become the head of the corner. Neither is there salvation in any other: for there is none other name under heaven given among men, whereby we must be saved. Now when they saw the boldness of Peter and John, and perceived that they were unlearned and ignorant men, they marvelled; and they took knowledge of them, that they had been with Jesus. (Acts 4:1-13)

When you receive the baptism of the Holy Ghost, the boldness to declare the counsel of the Lord is manifested. This happened to Peter, who when confronted by the rulers of the people over which power the Apostles were using to cast out unclean spirits, was able to answer boldly without being intimidated.

One might not appreciate this event until you compare it with what happened in John 18:15-15 "*And Simon Peter followed Jesus, and so did another disciple: that disciple was known unto the high priest, and went in with Jesus into the palace of the high priest. But Peter stood at the door without. Then went out that other disciple, which was known unto the high priest, and spake unto her that kept the door, and brought in Peter. Then saith the damsel that kept the door unto Peter, Art not thou also one of this man's disciples? He saith, I am not.*"

Before the little damsel who had confronted him, Peter denied Jesus but now, after the Holy Spirit had come upon him, he had received a supernatural boldness. Standing before the rulers of the people who had power to terminate his life, he preached the gospel of Jesus boldly without any fear.

When the Holy Ghost comes upon a man, timidity gives way to boldness.

5. Giving enabled by the Holy Spirit

And when they had prayed, the place was shaken where they were assembled together; and they were all filled with the Holy Ghost, and they spake the word of God with boldness. And the multitude of them that believed were of one heart and of one soul: neither said any of them that ought of the things which he possessed was his own; but they had all things common.

And with great power gave the apostles witness of the resurrection of the Lord Jesus: and great grace was upon them all. Neither was there any among them that lacked: for as many as were possessors of lands or houses sold them, and brought the prices of the things that were sold, and laid them down at the apostles' feet: and distribution was made unto every man according as he had need.

And Joses, who by the apostles was surnamed Barnabas, (which is, being interpreted, The son of consolation,) a Levite, and of the country of Cyprus, having land, sold it, and brought the money, and laid it at the apostles' feet. (Acts 4:31-37)

The Holy Ghost enables liberality in giving. There is a way a believer gains deeper insight into stewardship and the management of material possessions when he is baptized in the Holy Ghost. He begins to realize that no man receives anything except what is given from above.

His focus changes from chasing after earthly possessions to pursuing the fulfillment of heavenly goals. His concerns in life move from his well being to that of others around him and how the name of the Lord will be glorified through him. When a believer still holds back material things, it is a sign that he is not yet fully broken and does not have knowledge of spiritual things.

6. Exposure and Judgment of Ananias and Saphira

But a certain man named Ananias, with Sapphira his wife, sold a possession, and kept back part of the price, his wife also being privy to it, and brought a certain part, and laid it at the apostles' feet.

But Peter said, Ananias, why hath Satan filled thine heart to lie to the Holy Ghost, and to keep back part of the price of the land? Whiles it remained, was it not thine own? and after it was sold, was it not in thine own power? why hast thou conceived this thing in thine heart? thou hast not lied unto men, but unto God. And Ananias hearing these words fell down, and gave up the ghost: and great fear came on all them that heard these things. And the young men arose, wound him up, and carried him out, and buried him. And it was about the space of three hours after, when his wife, not knowing what was done, came in.

And Peter answered unto her, Tell me whether ye sold the land for so much? And she said, Yea, for so much. Then Peter said unto her, How is it that ye have agreed together to tempt the Spirit of the Lord? behold, the feet of them which have buried thy husband are at the door, and shall carry thee out.

Then fell she down straightway at his feet, and yielded up the ghost: and the young men came in, and found her dead, and, carrying her forth, buried her by her husband. And great fear came upon all the church, and upon as many as heard these things. (Acts 5:1-11)

People have been playing games with God for a long time. However, the truth is that *God cannot be mocked, whatsoever a man sows, so shall he reap.* When the Holy Ghost is in charge several things happen. First, the presence of God is manifested. Second, it is impossible for the evil secrets of men to go unexposed and thirdly, nothing unholy can be accommodated.

The couple made a vow to sell their possessions and bring the proceeds thereof to the Apostle's feet. They sold their possessions but held back part of the proceeds. Peter, at the prompting of the Holy Ghost, said to the husband in verses 3 and 4 "*Ananias, why hath Satan filled thine heart to lie to the Holy Ghost, and to keep back part of the price of the land? Whiles it remained, was it not thine own? and after it was sold, was it not in thine own power? why hast thou conceived this thing in thine heart? thou hast not lied unto men, but unto God.*"

These two verses of the Bible easily drive home some powerful truths about God's expectations from His children:

- When a believer lies to another believer or to a group of believers or church, he has lied against the Holy Ghost.

- Whatever may lie within your power to do to other men, truth or truthfulness should be your first priority.

- Absolute sincerity to men is equal to absolute sincerity to God.

The couple conspired and lied to God and thereafter, one after the other, they lost their lives because they deceived God and underestimated the power of the Holy Ghost to discover the hidden secrets of men.

In the presence of the Holy Ghost, everything that is hidden shall be exposed. In our dealings with God and men, transparency is the watchword.

7. Gamaliel testifies of the power of God

And by the hands of the apostles were many signs and wonders wrought among the people; (and they were all with one accord in Solomon's porch. And of the rest durst no man join himself to them: but the people magnified them. And believers were the more added to the Lord, multitudes both of men and women.) Insomuch that they brought forth the sick into the streets, and laid them on beds and couches, that at the least the shadow of Peter passing by might overshadow some of them.

There came also a multitude out of the cities round about unto Jerusalem, bringing sick folks, and them which were vexed with unclean spirits: and they were healed every one. Then the high priest rose up, and all they that were with him, (which is the sect of the Sadducees,) and were filled with indignation,
And laid their hands on the apostles, and put them in the common prison. But the angel of the Lord by night opened the prison doors, and brought them forth, and said, Go, stand and speak in the temple to the people all the words of this life.

And when they heard that, they entered into the temple early in the morning, and taught. But the high priest came, and they that were with him, and called the council together, and all the senate of the children of Israel, and sent to the prison to have them brought.

But when the officers came, and found them not in the prison, they returned, and told, saying, the prison truly found we shut with all safety, and the keepers standing without before the doors: but when we had opened, we found no man within.

Now when the high priest and the captain of the temple and the chief priests heard these things, they doubted of them whereunto this would grow. Then came one and told them, saying, Behold, the men whom ye put in prison are standing in the temple, and teaching the people. Then went the captain with the officers, and brought them without violence: for they feared the people, lest they should have been stoned.

And when they had brought them, they set them before the council: and the high priest asked them, saying, Did not we straitly command you that ye should not teach in this name? and, behold, ye have filled Jerusalem with your doctrine, and intend to bring this man's blood upon us.

Then Peter and the other apostles answered and said, We ought to obey God rather than men. The God of our fathers raised up Jesus, whom ye slew and hanged on a tree. Him hath God exalted with his right hand to be a Prince and a Savior, for to give repentance to Israel, and forgiveness of sins. And we are his witnesses of these things; and so is also the Holy Ghost, whom God hath given to them that obey him. When they heard that, they were cut to the heart, and took counsel to slay them.

Then stood there up one in the council, a Pharisee, named Gamaliel, a doctor of the law, had in reputation among all the people, and commanded to put the apostles forth a little space; And said unto them, Ye men of Israel, take heed to yourselves what ye intend to do as touching these men. For before these days rose up Theudas, boasting himself to be somebody; to whom a number of men, about four hundred, joined themselves: who was slain; and all, as many as obeyed him, were scattered, and brought to nought.

After this man rose up Judas of Galilee in the days of the taxing, and drew away much people after him: he also perished; and all, even as many as obeyed him, were dispersed. And now I say unto you, Refrain from these men, and let them alone: for if this counsel or this work be of men, it will come to nought:

But if it be of God, ye cannot overthrow it; lest haply ye be found even to fight against God. And to him they agreed: and when they had called the apostles, and beaten them, they commanded that they should not speak in the name of Jesus, and let them go.

And they departed from the presence of the council, rejoicing that they were counted worthy to suffer shame for his name. And daily in the temple, and in every house, they ceased not to teach and preach Jesus Christ.

(Acts 5:12-42)

When the gospel is preached with power, many signs and wonders will follow. Many miracles were witnessed in the days of the Apostles because the work of the ministry was carried out under the complete control and influence of the Holy Ghost. Whenever God uses you to be a blessing to the lost, you will definitely attract the wrath of evil men.

The Apostles were thrown into jail but God intervened and the prison gates opened on their own accord and the Apostles were released to go back into the temple to preach the gospel. This caused a lot of confusion among the rulers of the land for they had not seen anything like that before and they attempted to re-arrest the Apostles but the Holy Ghost came upon a heathen Doctor of Law by the name Gamaliel and he spoke against their arrest pointing the attention of the rulers to the uniqueness of the Apostles and the futility of laying hands of them.

When you partner with the Holy Ghost, he can use anyone or any vessel to speak for you before the authorities. Your protection is supernaturally guaranteed.

8. Tabitha raised from the dead

Now there was at Joppa a certain disciple named Tabitha, which by interpretation is called Dorcas: this woman was full of good works and alms and deeds which she did.

And it came to pass in those days, that she was sick, and died: whom when they had washed, they laid her in an upper chamber.

And forasmuch as Lydda was nigh to Joppa, and the disciples had heard that Peter was there, they sent unto him two men, desiring him that he would not delay to come to them.

Then Peter arose and went with them. When he was come, they brought him into the upper chamber: and all the widows stood by him weeping, and shewing the coats and garments which Dorcas made, while she was with them.

But Peter put them all forth, and kneeled down, and prayed; and turning him to the body said, Tabitha, arise. And she opened her eyes: and when she saw Peter, she sat up.

And he gave her his hand, and lifted her up, and when he had called the saints and widows, presented her alive.

And it was known throughout all Joppa; and many believed in the Lord.

And it came to pass, that he tarried many days in Joppa with one Simon a tanner.

(Acts 9:36-43)

One could imagine the surprise and shock on the faces of the disciples when Jesus raised Lazarus from the dead in the book of John Chapter 11. They could have imagined that Jesus was the only one that had such power. However, when Jesus was getting ready to leave, He told them in John 14:12 "*Verily, verily, I say unto you, He that believeth on me, the works that I do shall he do also; and greater works than these shall he do; because I go unto my Father.*"

Not too long after the departure of Jesus, the same Peter was confronted with a dead woman called Tabitha. In verse 40, just like Jesus did with

Lazarus, he knelt down, prayed and commanded life to come back into the lifeless body of Tabitha and she came back to life immediately.

Any believer filled with the Holy Ghost can do what Peter did and even a faith as small as a mustard seed can bring about such great miracles.

When you partner with the Holy Ghost, there is nothing that shall be impossible to you to do.

9. Prison gates opened on their own accord

And when Herod would have brought him forth, the same night Peter was sleeping between two soldiers, bound with two chains: and the keepers before the door kept the prison.

And, behold, the angel of the Lord came upon him, and a light shined in the prison: and he smote Peter on the side, and raised him up, saying, Arise up quickly. And his chains fell off from his hands.

And the angel said unto him, Gird thyself, and bind on thy sandals. And so he did. And he saith unto him, Cast thy garment about thee, and follow me.

And he went out, and followed him; and wist not that it was true which was done by the angel; but thought he saw a vision.

When they were past the first and the second ward, they came unto the iron gate that leadeth unto the city; which opened to them of his own accord: and they went out, and passed on through one street; and forthwith the angel departed from him.

And when Peter was come to himself, he said, Now I know of a surety, that the Lord hath sent his angel, and hath delivered me out of the hand of Herod, and from all the expectation of the people of the Jews.

(Acts12:6-11)

When you work with the Holy Ghost, no human limitation can hold you down. No prison door can cage you in and no weapon that is formed against you shall prosper. God will certainly supernaturally deliver His own from every captivity of the enemy. You have to put your trust in the One that has called you that He will make all things beautiful in His time.

10. The lame walked

And there they preached the gospel. And there sat a certain man at Lystra, impotent in his feet, being a cripple from his mother's womb, who never had walked: The same heard Paul speak: who steadfastly beholding him, and perceiving that he had faith to be healed, Said with a loud voice, Stand upright on thy feet. And he leaped and walked. And when the people saw what Paul had done, they lifted up their voices, saying in the speech of Lycaonia, The gods are come down to us in the likeness of men. (Acts 14:7-11)

Every child of God must pay attention to God's gifting in his or her life. There is no man that is saved and baptized in the Holy Ghost that does not have at least one gift of the spirit. You must discover, develop and dispatch your gifts to a sick and needy world.

In 1 Corinthians 12:7-11, the Bible says *"But the manifestation of the Spirit is given to every man to profit withal. For to one is given by the Spirit the word of wisdom; to another the word of knowledge by the same Spirit; To another faith by the same Spirit; to another the gifts of healing by the same Spirit; To another the working of miracles; to another prophecy; to another discerning of spirits; to another divers kinds of tongues; to another the interpretation of tongues: But all these worketh that one and the selfsame Spirit, dividing to every man severally as he will."*

The Apostles of old had a deep understanding of this truth and they did these three things carefully, diligently and continuously:

Discover, develop and dispatch.

Whenever and wherever the true gospel is being preached, signs and wonders will confirm that the gospel is true. In the above story, the impotent man had Paul preached the gospel and through the word that was preached, faith developed in the heart of the impotent man. And Paul perceived what was happening in the man's heart and seized the moment to minister healing to the man and the man received his healing.

When we preach the gospel under the anointing of the Holy Ghost, healing, miracles, signs and wonders will definitely follow. This gospel has the capacity to make global impact.

11. The devil cast out of a damsel

And it came to pass, as we went to prayer, a certain damsel possessed with a spirit of divination met us, which brought her masters much gain by soothsaying: The same followed Paul and us, and cried, saying, These men are the servants of the most high God, which shew unto us the way of salvation. And this did she many days. But Paul, being grieved, turned and said to the spirit, I command thee in the name of Jesus Christ to come out of her. And he came out the same hour. And when her masters saw that the hope of their gains was gone, they caught Paul and Silas, and drew them into the marketplace unto the rulers, And brought them to the magistrates, saying, These men, being Jews, do exceedingly trouble our city, And teach customs, which are not lawful for us to receive, neither to observe, being Romans. And the multitude rose up together against them: and the magistrates rent off their clothes, and commanded to beat them. And when they had laid many stripes upon them, they cast them into prison, charging the jailor to keep them safely: Who, having received such a charge, thrust them into the inner prison, and made their feet fast in the stocks. (Acts 16:16-24)

The discerning of the spirits is one of the gifts of the Spirit that has been neglected by the body of Christ. In the church, the devil hides in human vessels to disguise as an angel of light until those gifted with discerning spirit rise up to the occasion. What the damsel was saying was the truth, however it took discernment by Paul to know that a demonic spirit had possessed the vessel speaking.

Many people these days are being deceived by the talk and speeches of men just because their words sounded like the truth. Fake Evangelists, fake prophets, fake teachers and fake Pastors abound in our times. It takes discernment by the church to expose this great wickedness so that the true and pure gospel can thrive and this can only happen when our churches partner with the Holy Ghost.

12. The earthquake visitation

And at midnight Paul and Silas prayed, and sang praises unto God: and the prisoners heard them.

And suddenly there was a great earthquake, so that the foundations of the prison were shaken: and immediately all the doors were opened, and every one's bands were loosed.

And the keeper of the prison awaking out of his sleep, and seeing the prison doors open, he drew out his sword, and would have killed himself, supposing that the prisoners had been fled.

But Paul cried with a loud voice, saying, Do thyself no harm: for we are all here.

Then he called for a light, and sprang in, and came trembling, and fell down before Paul and Silas, and brought them out, and said, Sirs, what must I do to be saved? And they said, Believe on the Lord Jesus Christ, and thou shalt be saved, and thy house.

And they spake unto him the word of the Lord, and to all that were in his house. And he took them the same hour of the night, and washed their stripes; and was baptized, he and all his, straightway. (Acts 16:25-33)

The key lesson in this story is how the gospel can bring the world to its feet. In verse 30, the keeper of the prison, who in our world represents the keeper of the law or the government of this world, said *"Sirs, what must I do to be saved?'.*

The church in partnership with the Holy Ghost can earn great respect from the authorities of this world by uncompromisingly preaching and demonstrating the power of the gospel. The world is tired of a 'routine church' and in dire need of an impactful movement that can bring the world and the powers in it to their feet. The Apostles responded immediately by leading the man to Christ and in verse 33, the Bible says *"And he took them the same hour of the night, and washed their stripes; and was baptized, he and all his, straightway."* Without soliciting, the man himself *"washed their stripes."*

Authorities in this world can "wash the stripes" of the church if they see the raw demonstration of the Holy Ghost power in the church. The church must denounce its beggarly and patronizing posture. The church is the light of the world and darkness cannot comprehend the light. But for that to happen, light must continue to be light. The light of the church cannot afford to be dim or else the *powers that be* in our world will look down, disrespect and disdain the church.

13. Fake spirits exposed and disgraced

And God wrought special miracles by the hands of Paul: so that from his body were brought unto the sick handkerchiefs or aprons, and the diseases departed from them, and the evil spirits went out of them. Then certain of the vagabond Jews, exorcists, took upon them to call over them which had evil spirits the name of the Lord Jesus, saying, we adjure you by Jesus whom Paul preacheth.

And there were seven sons of one Sceva, a Jew, and chief of the priests, which did so. And the evil spirit answered and said, Jesus I know, and Paul I know; but who are ye?

And the man in whom the evil spirit was leaped on them, and overcame them, and prevailed against them, so that they fled out of that house naked and wounded. And this was known to all the Jews and Greeks also dwelling at Ephesus; and fear fell on them all, and the name of the Lord Jesus was magnified. And many that believed came, and confessed, and shewed their deeds. (Acts 19:11-18)

What makes the name of Christ to work wonders in your life is the relationship you have with him. The Bible says in Mark 16:15-18 *"And he said unto them, Go ye into the entire world, and preach the gospel to every creature. He that believeth and is baptized shall be saved; but he that believeth not shall be damned. And these signs shall follow them that believe; In my name shall they cast out devils; they shall speak with new tongues; They shall take up serpents; and if they drink any deadly thing, it shall not hurt them; they shall lay hands on the sick, and they shall recover."*

Proverbs 18:10 says *"The name of the Lord is a strong tower: the righteous runneth into it, and is safe."* Only the righteous has the right to call and use the name.

It is only the saved (the righteous) that can legitimately use the name of the Lord to do miracles. Signs that follow salvation are for the believer to cast out devils using the name of Jesus and the devils have no choice but to be cast out.

John 10:27 says *"My sheep hear my voice, and I know them, and they follow me."*

It is not only Jesus that knows his own, the evil spirits also know those who are His and those who are not His. When the sevens sons of Sceva saw what the Apostles were doing in the name of Jesus, they thought just anyone could do the same. However, the unclean spirits spoke back to them saying that they simply did not respond to every voice. Do the devils recognize who you are? When you partner with the Holy Ghost, He will use you to do the miraculous. To this particular day, devils are still being cast out through the name of Jesus.

14. Several healings

In the same quarters were possessions of the chief man of the island, whose name was Publius; who received us, and lodged us three days courteously. And it came to pass, that the father of Publius lay sick of a fever and of a bloody flux: to whom Paul entered in, and prayed, and laid his hands on him, and healed him.

So when this was done, others also, which had diseases in the island, came, and were healed: Who also honored us with many honors; and when we departed, they laded us with such things as were necessary. (Acts 28:7-10)

Mark 16:18b says *"they shall lay hands on the sick, and they shall recover."* Paul demonstrated the healing power in the name of Jesus by laying hands on the sick father of his host and he got healed. Why are we not seeing much of this among present day believers? Part of the problem is lack of faith. We have a mental knowledge of the word but not an experiential knowledge of it. Your believing is never complete until there is a proof produced from what you believe and the more proofs you have the greater your faith becomes.

15. The gospel preached unhindered

And when they had appointed him a day, there came many to him into his lodging; to whom he expounded and testified the kingdom of God, persuading them concerning

Jesus, both out of the law of Moses, and out of the prophets, from morning till evening. And some believed the things which were spoken, and some believed not.

And when they agreed not among themselves, they departed, after that Paul had spoken one word, Well spake the Holy Ghost by Esaias the prophet unto our fathers, saying, Go unto this people, and say, Hearing ye shall hear, and shall not understand; and seeing ye shall see, and not perceive:

For the heart of this people is waxed gross, and their ears are dull of hearing, and their eyes have they closed; lest they should see with their eyes, and hear with their ears, and understand with their heart, and should be converted, and I should heal them.

Be it known therefore unto you, that the salvation of God is sent unto the Gentiles, and that they will hear it. And when he had said these words, the Jews departed, and had great reasoning among themselves. And Paul dwelt two whole years in his own hired house, and received all that came in unto him, Preaching the kingdom of God, and teaching those things which concern the Lord Jesus Christ, with all confidence, no man forbidding him. (Acts 28:23-31)

Romans 10:13-14 reads, *"For whosoever shall call upon the name of the Lord shall be saved. How then shall they call on him in whom they have not believed? and how shall they believe in him of whom they have not heard? and how shall they hear without a preacher?"*

Mark 16:15 also reads, *"Go ye into the entire world, and preach the gospel to every creature."*

Until believers step out of their comfort zone to preach the gospel, the power of the gospel cannot be confirmed. Paul admonishing young Timothy in 2 Timothy 4:1-5 saying *"I charge thee therefore before God, and the Lord Jesus Christ, who shall judge the quick and the dead at his appearing and his kingdom; preach the word; be instant in season, out of season; reprove, rebuke, exhort with all longsuffering and doctrine. For the time will come when they will not endure sound doctrine; but after their own lusts shall they heap to themselves teachers, having itching ears; And they shall turn away their ears from the truth, and shall be turned unto fables. But watch thou in all things, endure afflictions, do the work of an evangelist, make full proof of thy ministry."*

From the above scriptures we can clearly see that preaching the gospel is not just the work of Pastors and Evangelists. Everyone that is saved has a unique responsibility to preach the gospel and to emphasize sound doctrine. Many times the gospel will not be popular to the hearers especially the unsaved ones but as believers we must commit to preaching the true gospel because our world can only be saved through the preaching of the truth.

When we preach the gospel we should not be too bothered if all will believe or not. In the days of Paul, some believed and some did not. Our responsibility is to preach and it is the Holy Ghost that will convict the hearers to believe.

Chapter 6
Power in the overcoming life

⚜

W e live in dangerous times that require the church to rise up in
her full strength, in the glory and power of the Holy Spirit, to
take her place once again at the forefront of events. It is time to stretch
beyond playing church, lifeless sermons and irrelevant doctrines. As a
believer, you simply cannot live your life without fully understanding
the ministry of the Holy Spirit. It is a partnership that takes you beyond
your limitations and generates divine solutions.

Through the Holy Spirit, you have access to divine wisdom that will
cause you to shine both at home and at the workplace. God wants you
to be relevant in your world. You are indeed the salt of the earth and
the light of the world.

Without you, your world would grope in darkness. So many Christians
live like the world, chasing after temporary pleasures, complaining

like the world and many, unfortunately, die without leaving a legacy, without impacting their world, without touching their community. God has not called us to a life of mediocrity and He certainly did not save you simply for you to stay quiet and watch your world go to hell.

Going into partnership with the Spirit of God is the solution. This agreement or pact will propel you to live a life above and beyond the ordinary. The apostles and disciples were anything but ordinary. They shook the cities they stepped into and stunned leaders and local people alike. They carried raw power that simply was too powerful to go unnoticed.

You are a carrier of God's divine Spirit, which enables you to access the deep things of God. You are called to live a life of great impact and influence. You are made for a time such as this. The empowerment of the Holy Spirit will cause you to shine in every area of life. You simply need to surrender yourself to His guidance. This is the compelling truth that will change your life forever if you can grasp it. It is called "Divine Partnership."

Divine Partnership

I am the true vine, and my Father is the husbandman. Every branch in me that beareth not fruit he taketh away: and every branch that beareth fruit, he purgeth it, that it may bring forth more fruit. Now ye are clean through the word which I have spoken unto you.

Abide in me, and I in you. As the branch cannot bear fruit of itself, except it abide in the vine; no more can ye, except ye abide in me. I am the vine, ye are the branches: He that abideth in me, and I in him, the same bringeth forth much fruit: for without me ye can do nothing. (John 15:1-5)

What is partnership?

Partnership means two or more people working together for their mutual benefit. For example, a husband and wife may come together in order to produce children. A husband cannot produce a child alone and the wife cannot conceive a child by herself but when the two of them come together, a child can be born.

Likewise, in the case of divine partnership, it means God and man working together for their mutual benefit. Partnership in all ramifications is a contract of trust. When you sign the partnership contract with God, He expects you to trust him as a Senior Partner of the partnership. That is why the Bible says in Proverbs 3:5-8 "*Trust in the* Lord *with all thine heart; and lean not unto thine own understanding. In all thy ways acknowledge him, and he shall direct thy paths. Be not wise in thine own eyes: fear the* Lord, *and depart from evil. It shall be health to thy navel and marrow to thy bones.*"

The vine needs the branches and it is the branches that produce the fruits. The branches need the vine because without the vine, the branches can produce nothing. Of course, we know the branches need the vine more than the vine needs the branches. You see, when a branch is cut off, the vine produces other branches but if the vine is cut off, the whole plant dies.

Paraphrasing, I can say that I need God, God needs me, you need God and God needs you but the truth is that I need God more than He needs me, because if He says he wants to use me and I refuse, He has billions to choose from. When God says you should be in partnership with Him, He is simply saying let us walk together, for mutual benefit.

Biblical Examples of Divine Partnership

Here are two examples of divine partnership, one in the Old Testament and the other in the New Testament.

A.   Prophet Ezekiel in the valley of dry bones

1 The hand of the Lord was upon me, and carried me out in the spirit of the Lord, and set me down in the midst of the valley which was full of bones,

2 And caused me to pass by them round about: and, behold, there were very many in the open valley; and, lo, they were very dry.

3 And he said unto me, Son of man, can these bones live? And I answered, O Lord God, thou knowest.

4 Again he said unto me, Prophesy upon these bones, and say unto them, O ye dry bones, hear the word of the Lord.

5 Thus saith the Lord God unto these bones; Behold, I will cause breath to enter into you, and ye shall live:

6 And I will lay sinews upon you, and will bring up flesh upon you, and cover you with skin, and put breath in you, and ye shall live; and ye shall know that I am the Lord.

7 So I prophesied as I was commanded: and as I prophesied, there was a noise, and behold a shaking, and the bones came together, bone to his bone.

8 And when I beheld, lo, the sinews and the flesh came up upon them, and the skin covered them above: but there was no breath in them.

9 Then said he unto me, Prophesy unto the wind, prophesy, son of man, and say to the wind, Thus saith the Lord God; Come from the four winds, O breath, and breathe upon these slain, that they may live.

10 So I prophesied as he commanded me, and the breath came into them, and they lived, and stood up upon their feet, an exceeding great army.

(Ezekiel 37: 1-10)

Take note of a few things in the above verses of the Bible:

1. In verse 2, the Lord caused Ezekiel to go round about the valley of bones and he saw that they were very dry. God allows us to see the challenges and problems we are faced with. You cannot deal with a problem that you cannot see. Ezekiel did not just see bones; he saw bones that were dry.

2. In verse 3, the Lord did not call the bones dry. He only saw the bones the way they were originally made but it was Ezekiel who called them dry. God does not see our problems the way we see them. God asked Ezekiel "Can these bones live?" What you see about your problem is what it becomes. God needed to gauge the faith of Ezekiel before He could work with him. Hebrews 11:1 says *"Now faith is the substance of things hoped for, the evidence of things not seen."* Nothing happens when nothing is believed.

3. Ezekiel said, *"Thou knowest"* because nothing can happen to a problematic situation outsider the knowledge of God. Ezekiel was simply telling God "You know it can become whatever You want it to become after all You made it" or "You can fix it, even though I see it as dry, it is based on my limited knowledge which cannot be compared to your infinite knowledge."

4. Ezekiel understood divine partnership. The fulfillment of destiny is only made possible when there is a partnership between God and man.

5. As soon as God saw that Ezekiel had this understanding, He moved to the next stage of partnership. He commanded Ezekiel to "prophesy" - a word that means *"say what (a specific thing) will happen in the future."* God was plainly saying, "the future of these dry bones depends on what you say and not

only what I, God, knows."

6. God did not leave Ezekiel to determine the words to say. God told him what to say. Knowing that Ezekiel did not know the exact words to say, God simply did not want to gamble with the process. He commanded him to say thus *"O ye dry bones, hear the word of the Lord. Thus saith the Lord God unto these bones; Behold, I will cause breath to enter into you, and ye shall live: And I will lay sinews upon you, and will bring up flesh upon you, and cover you with skin, and put breath in you, and ye shall live; and ye shall know that I am the Lord."* (Ezekiel 37:4)

7. In verse 7, Ezekiel prophesied as he was commanded. This is called obedience. In Isaiah 1:19-20, the Bible says *"If ye be willing and obedient, ye shall eat the good of the land: But if ye refuse and rebel, ye shall be devoured with the sword: for the mouth of the Lord hath spoken it."* Many things have not changed in our lives because of disobedience to spiritual authority. Though the words might not make sense to Ezekiel, "he did as he was commanded."

8. God is a gradualist. The flesh and the sinews came together but there was no breath in them. God will not take you to the next level of breakthrough until you pass the present test. A lot of people want to see the results in an instant but the kingdom does not work like that. Isaiah 28:9-10 says *"Whom shall he teach knowledge? and whom shall he make to understand doctrine? them that are weaned from the milk, and drawn from the breasts. For precept must be upon precept, precept upon precept; line upon line, line upon line; here a little, and there a little."* You cannot compel God to allow you to run your own calendar. He is in charge, you are not.

9. God commanded him to prophesy to the winds to bring breath

to the bones and again, "he did as he was commanded" and what was the result?

…and the breath came into them, and they lived, and stood up upon their feet, an exceeding great army. (Ezekiel 37:10)

Exceeding results can only come from exceeding partnership.

B. Peter and his idle ship

1 And it came to pass, that, as the people pressed upon him to hear the word of God, he stood by the lake of Gennesaret,
2 And saw two ships standing by the lake: but the fishermen were gone out of them, and were washing their nets.
3 And he entered into one of the ships, which was Simon's, and prayed him that he would thrust out a little from the land. And he sat down, and taught the people out of the ship.
4 Now when he had left speaking, he said unto Simon, Launch out into the deep, and let down your nets for a draught.
5 And Simon answering said unto him, Master, we have toiled all the night, and have taken nothing: nevertheless at thy word I will let down the net.
6 And when they had this done, they inclosed a great multitude of fishes: and their net brake.
7 And they beckoned unto their partners, which were in the other ship, that they should come and help them. And they came, and filled both the ships, so that they began to sink.
8 When Simon Peter saw it, he fell down at Jesus' knees, saying, Depart from me; for I am a sinful man, O Lord.
9 For he was astonished, and all that were with him, at the draught of the fishes which they had taken:
10 And so was also James, and John, the sons of Zebedee, which were partners

with Simon. And Jesus said unto Simon, Fear not; from henceforth thou shalt catch men.

11 And when they had brought their ships to land, they forsook all, and followed him.

(Luke 5: 1-11)

Everything God puts in our hands was put there to accomplish a specific purpose. The Bible says in John 1:3, *"All things were made by him; and without him was not anything made that was made."* This scripture says that God made everything for a purpose though it is clear that not all things end up achieving their purposes.

In the above story, in Luke 5, we can see an event between Jesus and Simon. In the first seven verses of this story the following facts can be established:

1. Jesus was on a ministry assignment by the lake of Gennesaret and He needed something to use as a platform to preach. (Verse 1)

2. Two ships were empty because their owners gave up on them and were cleaning up their nets to close for the day. (Verse 2)

3. Jesus engaged one of them to carry out a purpose that was different from their original purpose of fishing. (Verse 2)

4. Simon, one of the owners of the empty ships, did not object to Jesus using his ship despite the frustration of the day. (Verse 3)

5. After finishing His divine assignment of teaching the multitude, without any mention of the bad fishing day from Simon, Jesus

commanded him "Launch out into the deep, and let down your nets for a draught." (Verse 4)

6. Simon immediately explained that the day did not seem like a good day for a great catch, after all they had to have known better than Jesus when it came to fishing. (Verse 5)

7. Simon responded saying, "Master, we have toiled all the night, and have taken nothing: nevertheless at thy word I will let down the net." They obeyed Jesus who was not a fisherman and in verse 6, "they caught a great multitude of fish and their net began to break." Their harvest was so much that they needed their idle partners to come and help them with the catch. Not only did their nets break, their ships began to sink. (Verse 7)

Several questions can easily come to mind:

First, how did Jesus know what to do to get a different result? Did he use a different net? Did he know how to fish better? Did he know the terrain better?

Part of the answers can be found in John 1:1-3:

In the beginning was the Word, and the Word was with God, and the Word was God. The same was in the beginning with God. All things were made by him; and without him was not any thing made that was made.

He made the fish. He made the waters where they live, He created the materials the ship and the nets were made from. He summoned all of them together on a day He wanted to demonstrate who was in charge and they went in the direction He wanted them to go.

Though what Jesus did was amazing, I want you to focus on the attitude of Simon and his partners. Note that:

1. They already gave up for the day. They must have concluded "It's one of those days."

2. They perfectly described their experience of the day when they said: "*Master, we have toiled all the night, and have taken nothing: nevertheless at thy word I will let down the net.*" (Luke 5:5)

    The dictionary defines toil as:

    Work extremely hard or incessantly to engage in difficult and continuous work To exert physical energy in order to carry out a task.

3. They did not ignore the instruction of Jesus who was better known as a preacher and teacher than a fisherman. They obeyed.

4. They got a different result that their toil could not give them.

I have a few questions to ask you.

1. Has your daily life become an endless toil?

2. Do you do so much and have little to show for it?

3. Are you about to park the ship of your life by the lakeside of life when the ship should be actively on the lake?

4. Are you tired of what you are doing right now and about to clean up your nets and close shop?

If your answer to any of the above questions is yes then you have a company in Simon and the sons of Zebedee. You might need to give the ship to the one who can make a better use of it. The same net in the hands of Jesus will get a better result than staying in your tired, clueless and discouraged hands. The same net that caught nothing might need to change hands and your life will definitely get a better result. Was that not what happened to Moses when he despised the rod in his hands until God turned it into His rod and used him to deliver the people of Israel from slavery?

Was that not what happened to the widow of Zarephat in 1 Kings 17 when all she had was a handful of meal in a barrel and a little oil in a cruse. But when she turned it over to Elijah, the Bible says in verse 16 *"And the barrel of meal wasted not, neither did the cruse of oil fail, according to the word of the LORD, which he spake by Elijah."* It all depends on who is in charge of your net. The same net, but in a different hand, can be used to achieve a different result. Your net must change hands!

See what happened after Simon witnessed the miracle. He experienced a spiritual turn around. I call it "Taking a turn."

When Simon Peter saw it, he fell down at Jesus' knees, saying, Depart from me; for I am a sinful man, O Lord. For he was astonished, and all that were with him, at the draught of the fishes which they had taken: And so was also James, and John, the sons of Zebedee, which were partners with Simon. And Jesus said unto Simon, Fear not; from henceforth thou shalt catch men. And when they had brought their ships to land, they forsook all, and followed him. (Luke 5:8-11)

There comes a time in our lives when we need to reflect on where we are coming from, what we are doing presently and where we need to go next. Sometimes it takes a divine encounter for one to take a detour. Often times, we are so caught up and neck deep into what we are doing that, regardless of the results we are getting, we still hang in there whereas God wants to redirect our lives. After the events that happened in Luke 5:1-7, Simon took a turn, left all and became a follower of Jesus. He took a turn and later became 'a rock' whose shadow healed the sick. A time will come in your life that you have to take a turn. Until you leave what made you look like a superstar and follow the counsel of the Almighty, you might not yet be ready to move to the next level.

Simon was hitherto catching physical fish and making a living out of it. He was an expert of a kind but experts too have down times. Until that day when his expertise failed him, he never knew he needed a turn. Whenever you make a turn induced by a divine encounter, it is divine promotion. Jesus told Simon in verse 10 "*Fear not; from henceforth thou shalt catch men*" which meant Jesus was saying, "You will redirect men's attention to me the same way I'm redirecting your attention from catching fish." Simon and his partners had a career change that they never bargained for. Verse 11 says "*And when they had brought their ships to land, they forsook all, and followed him.*"

They brought their ships from their natural market place to land. They parked their tools of business. They forsook all. They left the known for the unknown. These men risked their only source of livelihood. They did not consult their family members or seek the opinion of friends. They did not give Jesus' offer a long and deep thought. They simply followed. They made a turn and their lives never remained the same. Jesus placed a demand on their lives, their career, their future and they followed him.

Are you ready to make a turn in your own life? I guarantee that you will never regret that decision.

Conclusion
The life of the Spirit

To fully live an overcoming life in and by the Spirit, I encourage you to study again and again the truths presented in this book. It is important to have a strong foundation as you tap into the endless riches of God's Spirit. It is time to go beyond relying on your own strength.

There is a much better way to life than by living life solely on self-will. If you try to stand on your own strength, you will fall just like Paul and be a wretched man. When you, on your own, set your will to do good it is destined to fail. Your works become dead religion and amounts to self-worship because you are saying you can do it on your own and you do not need help; but the good news is Jesus can. Jesus already overcame the power of sin and the law of sin and death.

The law of the Spirit of life in Christ Jesus can be summarized in Philippians 4:13 *'I can do all things through Christ which strengtheneth me.'*

The better way is to humbly come to Christ. Come to the indwelling Christ in you and His power to release His power. Let Christ shine through your life. Paul said there is no good thing in his flesh but Christ dwells in us (**Get this revelation, if you are a believer then Christ is in you**) and He is truly good and wants to release all His goodness and love out of you. From you will flow rivers of living water. Amen!

Jesus lives in your spirit and Jesus has more than enough power to break the law or power of sin. Pray that power and light be released out of you! Rely upon and draw upon the law of the Spirit of life in Christ Jesus! If you tune into the truth that Christ dwells in you and lives in you, and you release Christ or His Spirit, you overcome evil. I can truly love others and overcome sin. Praise the Lord! Ask Jesus to flow through you and submit to His leading.

As believers, we are to 'die to self' and allow Christ to live through us. Note that is a daily experience. That is why Paul said in 1 Corinthians 15:31, "*I protest by your rejoicing which I have in Christ Jesus our Lord, I die daily.*"

Put away self-will and ask Jesus to release Himself through you to love, to have peace, joy, extend compassion and mercy to others, kindness and gentleness and to have patience and a sound mind. Self-will is opposed to Christ and Christianity. It is self-worship, dead works and pride, which will attract demonic powers. It brought Paul to a state of wretchedness and misery but Christ living in Paul and through Paul set Paul free. Paul developed a Christ-conscience not self-conscience. He allowed Christ to transform his mind and thinking. Christianity is not a self-improvement program. It is a total replacement program where we die and Christ lives in us. We are being transformed into the image of Christ and it is a process where Christ lives in us.

This is the new spiritual principle of life. It is through our vital union with Christ that we have received this life-giving Spirit. The Holy Spirit is the one who has a claim on our lives and the law no longer has any claim on the Christian because we have been made free from the law of sin and death.

New principles now control the Christian's life with new dynamics. We have found deliverance in the person and work of Jesus Christ. The law no longer has any jurisdiction over you! It can no longer lay any claim over you. We have been bought out of the slave market and made free to live this new life in Christ. God sent His Son to be our sin offering and die in our place to turn the wrath of God aside.

The difference between the life of the Christian and the life of the legalist is the believer lives a righteous life, not in the power of the law, but in the power of the Spirit of God. The law does not have the power to produce holiness in us. The only power it has is the ability to condemn.

As you yield to the control of the Holy Spirit, you will begin to experience the sanctifying work of the Spirit in your daily life. The righteous requirements of the law are fulfilled as you yield the control of your life to the Spirit. The righteous and just requirements of the law are fully met in us, who live and move and have our being in Christ.

The difference lies in who has control of our lives. Living the overcoming life means you are no longer controlled by the standards of the world but are now under the control of the Holy Spirit.

About the Author

Ezekiel Leke Ojo is the pastor of RCCG Solid Rock Phoenix located in the heart of Glendale, a church on the cutting edge of the end-time move to connect a dying world to a loving God.

He is the Provincial Pastor for Region 2 Province which comprises of The Redeemed Christian church of God, North America (RCCGNA) churches in Arizona, Washington, Oregon, Nevada, Utah and parts of Southern California. He was the Founding National Coordinator of the RCCGNA Young Adults and Singles ministry - a ministry set up to empower young adults and singles to fulfill their destinies and be relevant in today's world.

Ezekiel currently serves on the Board of African Missions North America; an organization set up to minister to millions of thirsty and needy souls in the forgotten corners of Africa and a member of the RCCGNA Strategic Team; an eight-member group set up to chart a course for the future of RCCGNA.

He ran a radio ministry broadcast tagged "Moment of Empowerment" in the state of Arizona and parts of Colorado and New Mexico between 2004 and 2007 and he is a regular host and speaker on TBN'S Praise the Lord program in Phoenix Arizona.

He is a passionate teacher of the word; addicted to praise and prayer and an unrepentant church planter who freely operates in apostolic gifts. A versatile preacher of the word, Ezekiel organizes year round prayer, leadership, mentoring and youth conferences all over the world; his passion is to empower and direct people from where they are to where God wants them to be and to get as many souls as possible to the kingdom.

He is a professional public Accountant and currently runs his practice in Phoenix, Arizona and Lagos, Nigeria. He is presently putting finishing touches to his PhD program in Business Administration at the North Central University, Prescott Arizona having bagged an MBA in Accounting and another Master's degree in Organizational Leadership from Grand Canyon University in Phoenix AZ where he also served as an Adjunct faculty.

An astute business man and entrepreneur, Ezekiel is the President/CEO of Joseph Generation Inc., a behavioral service company in the heart of Glendale Arizona and the Managing Partner of Leadright Consulting Inc, a leadership training and capacity development outfit with headquarters in Glendale Arizona. He is presently undergoing certification programs with two of the best in leadership and capacity development; the John Maxwell Organization and the Ken Blanchard organization both based in the US.

An alumnus of the University of Ilorin, Nigeria where he bagged a first degree in Economics. He is also a fellow of the Institute of Chartered Accountants of Nigeria, the Chartered Institute of Taxation of Nigeria and the Nigeria Institute of Management. He is the Managing Partner of Ezekiel Ojo & Co (Chartered Accountants); a Lagos based accounting and consulting practice. An International Associate of the American Institute of Certified Public Accountants, he is also a member of the Institute of Management Consultants of America.

He is happily married to Dr Juyi Ojo, a Registered Pharmacist and Pastor, their union is blessed with two children, David and Debbie. When he is not ministering, studying or impacting lives, he enjoys watching and analyzing soccer and global politics.

AVAILABLE NOW!

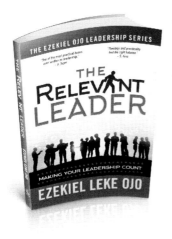

One of the greatest problems that the world is currently facing is the dearth of quality leadership to provide direction for our world, families, government, churches, and businesses. Name it. It is everywhere and there is a huge vacancy for capable hands to provide direction for a world that clearly needs leadership.

Leadership is beyond titles or positions. Leadership is said to be relevant when it is able to, at least, provide solutions to the problems that created a need for that leadership in the first place. Until that is done, leadership cannot be said to be relevant.

This book attempts to provide answers to key questions in leadership relevance. And these components are the leader's personal life, attitude, loyalty, credibility, motivation and equipping ability. This book is recommended as a teaching manual for anyone that occupies the position of a trainer, mentor, coach and leader.

Leadright Consulting Inc (LCI) was born out of a desire to fill some visible gaps in capacity development and leadership training in the corporate world. The vision for the company was given birth to as a result of obvious yearning for human resource enhancement and development in for-profit and nonprofit organizations.

The visionary, Ezekiel Ojo is a capacity development expert with over two decades of leadership experience spanning over three continents in six different industries.

We also engage in global tutoring and facilitation of professional accounting examinations in under-represented parts of the world especially Africa. We intend to bring the training and examination of professional accounting bodies to the under-served countries of the world. Main focus will be on CPA, CMA and CIA exams.

Leadright Consulting Inc. is affiliated to John Maxwell Organization and Ken Blanchard Organization; two of the world's most renowned leadership and capacity development organizations. *Visit* www.leadrightconsulting.com